TO

_____

FROM

_____

DATE

_____

VeggieTales

MY
TIME
with
GOD

365
Daily Devos
for Boys

veggietales.com

WORTHY®
kids

ISBN: 978-1-5460-1460-7 (paperback)
ISBN: 978-1-5460-1459-1 (padded hardcover)

WorthyKids
Hachette Book Group
1290 Avenue of the Americas, New York, NY 10104

WorthyKids is a division of Hachette Book Group, Inc. The WorthyKids name and logo are trademarks of Hachette Book Group, Inc.

Printed and bound in China
RRD-S
10 9 8 7 6 5 4 3 2 1

VeggieTales

MY TIME with GOD

365 Daily Devos for Boys

A NOTE TO PARENTS OR GRANDPARENTS

As a parent or grandparent, you know the importance of teaching children the big ideas that are found in God's Word and encouraging them to spend time with Him. The daily devotions in this book will help you do that.

Each entry contains a Bible verse and a kid-friendly devotion on an important topic such as honesty, forgiveness, or kindness. A question or thought follows to reinforce the message for the day, and a daily prayer will help your child to develop a habit of talking to God.

During the coming year, encourage your son or grandson to read a devotion from this book every day. This will help him establish a daily practice of hearing from God. It will also provide 365 opportunities to share God's love and wisdom and a daily chance for him to be reminded that God made him special—He knows him so well and loves him very much.

A GIFT FROM GOD

For by grace you have been saved through faith. And this is not your own doing; it is the gift of God.

EPHESIANS 2:8 ESV

Do you like presents? What's the best present you ever got? The Bible tells us about a wonderful gift God gives to each of His children. He gives us a place in His family forever!

God tells us all we have to do to receive this amazing gift is trust in Him and believe that He loves us. This is called *faith*. When you have faith in God, He promises to be with you always. Then you will never need to feel alone or afraid again. Isn't that the most wonderful gift you can imagine?

THOUGHT OF THE DAY

God's gifts are the best. Trust Him, and He'll take care of the rest!

PRAY TODAY

Dear God, thank You for giving me the gift of faith so I can trust in You and live with You forever. Amen.

WHAT CAN YOU DO?

"There's a youngster here with five barley loaves and a couple of fish! But what good is that with all this mob?"

JOHN 6:9 TLB

This Bible verse is about a time when a child gave Jesus his small lunch and Jesus multiplied it to make enough to feed thousands of people. Do you ever feel like you can't help others because you are just a child? If you ask Jesus to take what you *do* have and help you share it, He will. Maybe you can give some of your toys or books to children who don't have any. Maybe you can make a picture for someone who is lonely. Your small gift might make a BIG difference to someone! Ask Jesus how you can help. He will help you find a way.

THOUGHT OF THE DAY

Who needs your help today? What can you do?

PRAY TODAY

Dear God, thank You for giving me so much. Please help me to find ways to help others. Amen.

GOD'S TREASURE MAP

All Scripture is inspired by God and is useful to teach us what is true.

2 TIMOTHY 3:16 NLT

Have you ever pretended to go on a treasure hunt? Maybe you even made a treasure map! Do you know that the Bible is like a treasure map? It is filled with exciting stories about brave men and women. It contains directions on how to find treasures like joy, peace, and faith. In its pages, you can discover wonderful truths like God's amazing love for you. When you have a question or a problem, the Bible always has the best answer. So start reading your Bible now—you never know what treasures you might find!

THOUGHT OF THE DAY

Ask your parents if you can have a weekly family time where you read from the Bible together and talk about what you learn.

PRAY TODAY

Dear God, thank You for giving me the treasure of Your Word. Help me to read it, believe it, and follow it every day. Amen.

GOD'S GOOD PLANS

"I know that you can do all things. No plan of yours can be ruined."

JOB 42:2 ICB

Have you ever planned to play with a friend, but then your friend got sick? Or maybe you planned to go to the park, but then it rained and you couldn't go. Our plans don't always work out because we can't control everything. But God's plans always work out because God knows everything and He can do anything! There is no power that can stop God's plans. And because He loves you, God has good plans for you and your family. Even when your plans fail, you can be sure that God's plans will always work out.

THOUGHT OF THE DAY

You can always depend on God's good plans.

PRAY TODAY

Dear God, please help me to remember that You have wonderful plans for me. Thank You for loving me so much! Amen.

MORE THAN ANYTHING

"For this is how God loved the world: He gave his one and only Son, so that everyone who believes in him will not perish but have eternal life."

JOHN 3:16 NLT

God wants us to live with Him forever. But the only way that could happen was for God to send Jesus to give His life for us. So guess what? God sent Jesus, and Jesus chose to do it. He loves us more than anything—even more than His own life.

That kind of love is hard to understand, but don't worry. You don't have to understand it. You just have to accept it! That's all God wants.

So say a prayer thanking God for the incredible gift of Jesus. He loves you, now and forever, more than you can imagine.

THOUGHT OF THE DAY
Can you think of three ways God shows His love for you every day?

PRAY TODAY
Dear God, Your love is so big!
I may never understand it,
but I am so thankful for it.
And I love You too! Amen.

THE MOST POWERFUL

I ... pray that you will understand the incredible greatness of God's power for us who believe him.

EPHESIANS 1:19 NLT

God is more powerful than anyone or anything. He created the whole world. He makes the sun rise in the morning and the stars shine at night. He is strong enough to build mountains and control oceans. And His power can make you brave!

It's hard to be brave when you feel afraid. But God is always with you, and nothing is bigger than God. All you have to do is ask for His help! Pray for God to share His power with you. Then you can face anything!

THOUGHT OF THE DAY

Even when you feel weak, God is strong!

PRAY TODAY

Dear God, I'm glad You are more powerful than anything! Help me remember to trust Your power all the time. Amen.

LOVE OTHERS LIKE YOURSELF

"Just as you want others to do for you, do the same for them."

LUKE 6:31 HCSB

Jesus gives us an easy way to remember how to treat people. Think of how YOU want to be treated, and then just do that! If you want people to be kind to you, be kind to them. If you want others to share with you, share with them. It's that easy.

But sometimes it's *not* easy, is it? When someone is mean, it's hard to be nice in return. Remember that you can't control what anyone else does—but you *can* control what you do. Ask God to help you choose kindness and respect. You might just inspire others to do the same!

THOUGHT OF THE DAY

Always choose kindness. It just might come back to you!

PRAY TODAY

Dear God, I love when people are kind to me! Help me remember that other people want kindness and respect too. Amen.

NOTHING IS TOO HARD FOR GOD

"God can do anything!"

LUKE 1:37 NCV

Have you ever read the story of Moses? God did what seemed like the impossible through Moses! Moses rescued his people from a mean Egyptian king by separating the waters of a huge sea so they could walk across to the other side! Some of God's instructions must have seemed scary or strange, but God always knows what He is doing—and nothing is impossible for God!

God can do impossible things in your life too. If you have a problem that seems too hard to solve, go to God and trust Him. He is strong enough to do anything!

THOUGHT OF THE DAY

Can you think of another Bible story where God did something that seemed impossible?

PRAY TODAY

Dear God, You are so strong and wonderful! Thank You that I can come to You, no matter how big my questions are. Amen.

CHOOSING TO FORGIVE

Be gentle and ready to forgive; never hold grudges. Remember, the Lord forgave you, so you must forgive others. Most of all, let love guide your life.

COLOSSIANS 3:13–14 TLB

What if someone hurts your feelings, but then later says they're sorry? You have a choice: you can choose to stay mad or choose to forgive and be friends again. What would you do?

God says it is good to forgive others and not stay mad. It's not always easy, but we can ask God for help. Remember that God always forgives us when we are sorry for doing something wrong. He's the expert! And since He wants us to follow His ways, He can help us do just that. It's loving and kind to forgive, and it makes God happy too!

THOUGHT OF THE DAY

Saying "sorry" and forgiving is the way to happy living!

PRAY TODAY

Dear God, thank You for always forgiving me. Please help me to choose to forgive others. Amen.

GOD GIVES GOOD THINGS

For the LORD God is our sun and our shield. He gives us grace and glory. The LORD will withhold no good thing from those who do what is right.

PSALM 84:11 NLT

God always gives His children good things. He provides sunshine and rain so things can grow. He gives us families so that we can be loved. He gives us homes to live in so we can feel safe. He gives us bodies that can do many amazing things. He helps us learn and grow, sleep and play. And best of all, He gives us His love so that we can know Him and live with Him forever. God wants to give us every good thing because He is a loving Father to all His children!

THOUGHT OF THE DAY

Name three good things God has given you!

PRAY TODAY

Dear God, thank You so much for being my loving heavenly Father and for giving me so many good things. Amen.

A GREAT BIG FAMILY

"And I will be a father to you, and you shall be sons and daughters to me, says the Lord Almighty."

2 CORINTHIANS 6:18 ESV

Every family is different. Some are big, and some are small. Some live close together, while others are miles apart. But one thing should be important in every family: love!

Sometimes people don't feel a lot of love in their families. But here's good news: everyone can be in God's family! God is our Father, and He asks us to act like loving brothers and sisters. So let's look for ways to have fun together and take care of each other! In God's family, there's always enough love to go around.

THOUGHT OF THE DAY

How can you care for another member of God's family today?

PRAY TODAY

Dear God, thank You for my family and for making me part of Your family too! Amen.

BIG DREAMS

Now glory be to God, who by his mighty power at work within us is able to do far more than we would ever dare to ask or even dream of—infinitely beyond our highest prayers, desires, thoughts, or hopes.

EPHESIANS 3:20 TLB

Have you ever had big dreams about what you would like to be when you grow up? Maybe you dream about being a firefighter or a teacher or a dancer or an astronaut. The Bible says that God loves you, and He has big dreams for you too. He wants to help you have a wonderful life when you grow up! Because He made you, He knows what is best for you and how to help you. Stay close to God so that you and He will accomplish your big dreams together!

THOUGHT OF THE DAY

God has the power to make big dreams come true!

PRAY TODAY

Dear God, thank You for loving me and for giving me hope for a wonderful future with You! Amen.

GOD'S LOVE STICKS AROUND

But for those who honor the LORD, his love lasts forever, and his goodness endures for all generations.

PSALM 103:17 GNT

Can you remember a time when your feelings changed? Maybe your favorite color switched to something new. Maybe you got mad at your brother or sister, or you made a new friend.

Feelings change often, but God's love never changes! You can never make God love you less because His love doesn't depend on anything you do. He loves you all the time!

When we trust God's love and let it fill our hearts, we'll feel more loving too. Don't be surprised if you want to tell people about it. Everyone should know about God's amazing love!

THOUGHT OF THE DAY

You can honor God's love by sharing kind words and doing good deeds.

PRAY TODAY

Dear God, thank You that Your love is always the same. Help me share Your love with others. Amen.

TRAIN YOUR BRAIN

Fix your thoughts on what is true and good and right. Think about things that are pure and lovely, and dwell on the fine, good things in others. Think about all you can praise God for and be glad about.

PHILIPPIANS 4:8 TLB

Do you know you can see more good things just by thinking about good things? It's true! That's because when you focus on what is good and true, you're training your brain to look for those things everywhere! And the more you do it, the easier it gets.

If you want to make sure you're thinking good things, check in with your feelings. If you're feeling sad or scared or angry, your thoughts might need to change! Thank God for His goodness, and find something to be happy about. Even small things can make a big difference!

THOUGHT OF THE DAY

What is something that makes you happy right now? Praise God for it!

PRAY TODAY

Dear God, thank You for Your world! Please show me things to be glad about every day. Amen.

GOD'S BLESSINGS

You are wonderful . . . you store up blessings for all who honor and trust you.

PSALM 31:19 CEV

God is so good that He loves to give blessings to all of us. Blessings are wonderful gifts that only God can give. He gives us His words in the Bible so we can know Him and know how to live. He gives us friends and family so we can understand love and friendship. He gives us minds so we can think and learn and imagine. He gives us all these amazing things now, and He says that He has even more blessings stored up for us in heaven! Isn't that wonderful news?

THOUGHT OF THE DAY

Name some of the blessings you want to thank God for today!

PRAY TODAY

Dear God, thank You for all of the blessings You have given me. Help me always remember them. Amen.

PRAY FOR OTHERS

First of all, I ask you to pray for everyone. Ask God to help and bless them all, and tell God how thankful you are for each of them.

1 TIMOTHY 2:1 CEV

The Bible tells us that we can talk to God and pray for others. And you can talk to God about anything that's on your mind. In fact, God wants you to!

Praying for others is a great way to care for them. You can pray for people you know, like your family and friends, and you can also pray for people you've never met—even the president! After all, everyone needs God's help. So the next time you pray, think about who might need God's special care. Your prayers can bless other people in a big way.

THOUGHT OF THE DAY

Who can you pray for today? Say a prayer for them right now!

PRAY TODAY

Dear God, please be with all the people in my life and show them that You care for them! Amen.

FORGIVING MAKES THINGS BETTER

Be kind and compassionate to one another, forgiving each other, just as in Christ God forgave you.

EPHESIANS 4:32 NIV

Sometimes when we've done something wrong, we feel bad about it. We might want to hide or pretend we didn't do it, but that doesn't make the feeling go away. God makes a way for us to feel better. It is called forgiveness!

It's simple. You can go to the person you have hurt, tell them what you have done, and ask them to forgive you. When we say "sorry" and ask for forgiveness, we always feel better. God says that giving and receiving forgiveness are wonderful ways to show kindness to one another.

THOUGHT OF THE DAY

God forgives, and so should we!

PRAY TODAY

Dear God, thank You for forgiving me. Please help me ask for forgiveness when I have done something wrong. Amen.

FRIENDS YOU CAN TRUST

Friends come and friends go, but a true friend sticks by you like family.

PROVERBS 18:24 MSG

Bob and Larry are best friends. They always tell the truth, and most importantly, they like each other just the way they are. A best friend is someone you can really depend on!

Do you want to have a friend like that? You can start by being one! Tell the truth kindly. Encourage one another. And never share gossip—about each other or anyone else.

Remember that true friends will like you for you. They won't try to change you. When you spend time with people like that, you'll find friends who feel like family!

THOUGHT OF THE DAY

Who are some of your friends? What do you like about them?

PRAY TODAY

Dear God, thank You for the friends You've given me. Please help me to be a trustworthy, loving friend to each one. Amen.

SONGS FOR GOD

*Sing to the LORD a new song; sing to the LORD, all the earth.
Sing to the LORD and praise his name; every day tell how
he saves us.*

PSALM 96:1-2 NCV

The Bible is full of songs. Miriam sang to God after her brother Moses led the Israelites safely out of Egypt. Mary sang a song when she learned she would be Jesus' mother. And King David wrote many songs for God in the book of Psalms!

You can sing to God any time you want. Praise Him for all the great things He does! Sing a song to share your thoughts or even ask for help. Whether it's a favorite song from church or a song you just made up, sing it loud and proud. God loves to hear your voice!

THOUGHT OF THE DAY

Try adding a song to your prayers tonight!

PRAY TODAY

Dear God, sometimes I feel so happy, I just have to sing! Thank You for creating music so I can sing to You. Amen.

WORKING TOGETHER

Then make me truly happy by loving each other and . . . working together.

PHILIPPIANS 2:2 TLB

Have you ever had a really big task to do? If you have to do it by yourself, it might take a long time. But if someone helps you, the job is not only easier—it can even be fun! Working together makes things go faster too. You can learn new ways of doing something, make up a fun game, and maybe get to know someone better. When we work together, we are showing love and respect to one another. That's why it makes God so happy!

THOUGHT OF THE DAY

What are some things that are easier and more fun to do with someone else?

PRAY TODAY

Dear God, thank You for giving me friends and family so we can show our love by working together. Amen.

LEARN FROM YOUR MISTAKES

No one in this world always does right.

ECCLESIASTES 7:20 CEV

Nobody does everything right all the time. It isn't always easy to follow the rules in a new place or keep your temper or tell the truth. But here's some very good news: God is ready to forgive you and to help you learn from all of your mistakes! How did your actions or words make you feel? Do you need to apologize to someone? What can you do differently next time? A mistake is a perfect chance to keep growing into the person God wants you to be!

THOUGHT OF THE DAY

Everyone makes mistakes. But not everyone learns from them. Be sure you do!

PRAY TODAY

Dear God, sometimes it's hard to make good choices. Please help me learn from my mistakes! Amen.

LOOK AT THE GOOD

I said to myself, "Relax and rest. GOD has showered you with blessings."

PSALM 116:7 MSG

When things don't go the way you want, it's easy to feel upset. But here's a way to feel better: look at the good!

Everything God does is good. You can think about your family and friends. You can remember the times God has comforted you and helped you. And you can imagine the amazing plans He has for you. When you start thinking of all the good things in your life, bad things don't seem so big after all. So the next time you have a not-so-great day, look at the good! God's goodness makes everything better.

THOUGHT OF THE DAY

Good things from God are called "blessings." Try to count your blessings—you may have more than you think!

PRAY TODAY

Dear God, You've given me so many blessings! Help me remember them when I'm having a hard day. Amen.

TRACKING JESUS

For God called you to do good, even if it means suffering, just as Christ suffered for you. He is your example, and you must follow in his steps.

1 PETER 2:21 NLT

Some people know how to follow animals in the woods by "tracking" them. They understand how different animals act and can even find their footprints (or pawprints!) to figure out where they've been.

The Bible tells us to follow Jesus' steps. We can't see them like footprints in the snow, but we can get to know Jesus so well that we understand His ways. When you read Bible stories, think of what Jesus is like. How does He treat people? What's important to Him? Then every day, look for ways to be more like Him. That's how you follow Jesus!

THOUGHT OF THE DAY

Get better at "tracking" Jesus by reading about Him in the Bible.

PRAY TODAY

Dear God, I want to follow Jesus. Any time I have a choice to make, help me imagine what Jesus would do! Amen.

TRUSTING GOD

When I am afraid, I will trust in You.

PSALM 56:3 HCSB

What do you do when you are afraid? God knows that sometimes we will be afraid, but He doesn't want us to feel alone. That's why He tells us to trust in Him. Trusting in God means believing that what He says is true and knowing His love will never go away. A good way to do this is to remember a Bible verse and to say it when we are afraid. Words from the Bible are true, and they help us remember that God is always with us. Can you memorize the verse above? Then the next time you are afraid, you can say it out loud!

THOUGHT OF THE DAY

God's Word is true and trustworthy.

PRAY TODAY

Dear God, thank You for being with me when I'm afraid. I'm so glad I can always trust in You. Amen.

RUN TO FINISH WELL

Let us run the race that is before us and never give up.

HEBREWS 12:1 NCV

Have you ever run in a race? Some races are short, and other races are long; but every race has a finish line. In order to finish well, you need to keep running. If you quit, you won't get there!

The Bible says that life is a lot like a race. Some things take a short time—like helping at home or finishing homework. Other things take a long time—like learning to read or playing a sport. Just like in a race, you need to keep going in order to finish well!

THOUGHT OF THE DAY

What is something you'd like to get better at doing?

PRAY TODAY

Dear God, thank You for always being with me and helping me to finish well. Amen.

ASK FOR WISDOM

If any of you needs wisdom, you should ask God for it. God is generous. He enjoys giving to all people, so God will give you wisdom.

JAMES 1:5 ICB

Have you ever had a problem you couldn't figure out? Maybe you had an argument with someone, or you wanted to make a new friend. The Bible says that whenever we need wisdom—or don't know what to do—we can ask God, and He will help us. God knows everything. No problem is too hard for Him. Take time to pray, asking God for help next time you have to make a hard decision or solve a problem. Then listen for what He wants you to know. God wants to help you out!

THOUGHT OF THE DAY

What do you need wisdom for today?

PRAY TODAY

Dear God, I don't always know what to do or say. Please give me Your wisdom every day. Amen.

SHARE AND GIVE

Be generous, and someday you will be rewarded.

ECCLESIASTES 11:1 CEV

Jesus doesn't just ask us to give—He asks us to give *generously!* That means sharing all we have, even the things we really like.

What do you have to share? Can you split your lunch with a classmate who doesn't have one? Could you donate part of your allowance to your church or a local charity? Maybe you have some cool toys you could give to kids who don't have many toys of their own. It's not always easy to give up our stuff. But God promises that generosity is a blessing to everyone. So give giving a try. You might be surprised by how much you enjoy it!

THOUGHT OF THE DAY

When you share what you have, you give more than just things. You give joy!

PRAY TODAY

Dear Jesus, thank You for the blessings in my life! Please help me share what I have with others. Amen.

HOME SWEET HOME

"If a kingdom is divided against itself, that kingdom cannot stand. If a house is divided against itself, that house cannot stand."

MARK 3:24–25 NIV

Who lives with you in your home? Mom and Dad? Brothers and sisters? Grandparents or aunts and uncles? Family is one of God's most special gifts, and when everyone cares for each other, home is a fun and happy place!

Sometimes you might feel annoyed with someone in your family. That's normal! The important thing is to choose kind words, find ways to solve problems together, and apologize for hurt feelings right away. That way, everyone feels loved, safe, and supported. It's the kind of home God wants all of us to have!

THOUGHT OF THE DAY

How does your home make you feel?

PRAY TODAY

Dear God, thank You for my family. Please help us have fun and care for each other, even when we disagree! Amen.

SAYING THANKS

Praise the LORD. Give thanks to the LORD, for he is good; his love endures forever.

PSALM 106:1 NIV

When your mom or dad does something nice for you, you probably say thanks! When a friend shares a toy or gives you a gift, you say thanks too. But have you ever thought about saying thanks to God?

He is always good, He loves you, and He gives you wonderful things every day! God gives you family and friends, good food to eat, and a beautiful world where you can run and play. It makes God happy when His children take the time to say thanks for all He does. Will you do that today?

THOUGHT OF THE DAY
Think of three things you can thank God for right now!

PRAY TODAY
Dear God, thank You for loving me and for helping me every day. Amen.

KINDNESS STARTS WITH YOU

Therefore, as God's chosen people, holy and dearly loved, clothe yourselves with compassion, kindness, humility, gentleness and patience.

COLOSSIANS 3:12 NIV

Sometimes it's nice to let other people go before you. But God wants you to go first in one important thing: kindness!

The Bible tells us to think of kindness like clothing. It should be the first thing you put on every day, and everyone should be able to see it right away! When you choose to be nice first, you show people that you care about them. And you can be nice to *anyone*! So even if you think someone doesn't like you, or you don't know someone very well, you can take the first step. See what happens when kindness starts with you!

THOUGHT OF THE DAY

Pick someone to show kindness to today. Then be sure you go first!

PRAY TODAY

Dear God, please help me to be kind to everyone. I want it to be the first thing people notice about me! Amen.

THANK GOD FOR YOU

"You're blessed when you're content with just who you are—no more, no less."

MATTHEW 5:5 MSG

Have you ever wanted to be like someone else? Well, guess what? God never thinks that about you! He loves you for exactly who you are.

Everyone in the world has something different to give. Instead of focusing on what others can do, think about what makes you you. Do you like to draw? Are you a great listener? Do you notice small things or dream big dreams? What makes you laugh? Ask God to help you see all the things He loves about you. Then thank Him for every single one!

THOUGHT OF THE DAY

What are three things you like about yourself?

PRAY TODAY

Dear God, thank You for Your unending love! Help me to see myself the way You see me. Amen.

GROWING FAITH

So faith comes from hearing, that is, hearing the Good News about Christ.

ROMANS 10:17 NLT

The verse above says that faith, or believing, comes from hearing the Good News about Jesus. There are lots of ways to do that!

Maybe you go to Sunday school or church, where you listen to Bible stories and learn songs that tell you about God's love. When you read a devotional book like this one, you are also hearing the Good News. Reading the Bible and saying prayers before you eat or at bedtime help grow your faith too! Every day, try finding a few ways to help your faith get stronger and stronger.

THOUGHT OF THE DAY

What is your favorite way to learn about Jesus?

PRAY TODAY

Dear God, thank You for giving me so many ways to hear about Jesus and Your love for me! Please help my faith to grow. Amen.

SHOWING LOVE

Little children, let us stop just saying we love people; let us really love them, and show it by our actions.

1 JOHN 3:18 TLB

Did you know you can show people you love them without even using words? You can color a picture and give it to someone. You can help your siblings do their chores. You can give your mom a hug. There are so many ways to say "I love you" without saying a thing! The Bible says the best way to tell people you love them is to act with love and kindness. Can you think of ways to say "I love you" without saying a single word?

THOUGHT OF THE DAY

The very best way to say "I love you" is not with words, but with what you do!

PRAY TODAY

Dear God, please help me show Your love to others by using actions as well as words! Amen.

GROW IN GRACE

But grow in the grace and knowledge of our Lord and Savior Jesus Christ. To Him be the glory both now and forever. Amen.

2 PETER 3:18 NKJV

You know what it means to grow tall and strong. But God also wants us to grow in knowledge and grace. What does that mean?

You can grow in knowledge by learning new things. Listen to your Sunday school teacher, memorize verses, and read Bible stories at home to get to know God better. You can grow in grace by doing what God says and trusting that He loves you. The cool thing is that as you learn more about God, it gets easier to follow and trust Him. So you actually grow in knowledge and grace at the same time!

THOUGHT OF THE DAY

Pick a time each day to read your Bible.

PRAY TODAY

Dear God, thank You for Your love. Please help me grow in knowledge and grace every single day! Amen.

CONFIDENCE FROM GOD

For the LORD will be your confidence, and will keep your foot from being caught.

PROVERBS 3:26 ESV

Confidence is a big word that means "being sure you can do something." For example, once you learn how to count or spell or ride a bike, you can do those things with confidence.

But when you go to a new school, meet someone new, or try something for the first time, you might not feel very confident. That's OK, though, because the Lord says *He* will be your confidence! He is with you all the time, helping you to be brave even when you feel shy or scared. God will never let you down.

THOUGHT OF THE DAY

What is something you feel confident about? What would you like God to help you be more confident about?

PRAY TODAY

Dear God, thank You for staying close to me. Please help me trust You to give me confidence. Amen.

QUICK TO FORGIVE

"I will forgive their sins and will no longer remember their wrongs."

HEBREWS 8:12 GNT

When you say unkind words or choose not to follow the rules, it doesn't feel very good, does it? But here's some good news: you can always ask God to forgive you. And He always will!

God forgives you the moment you ask Him, and He'll fill you with His love. He will also give you courage and strength to do better the next time. His love and patience never run out. So be honest when you've made a mistake! God is always ready to forgive.

THOUGHT OF THE DAY
God forgives, no questions asked!

PRAY TODAY
Dear God, thank You that You always forgive me! When I make mistakes, help me ask for forgiveness right away. Amen.

LISTEN AND ACT!

But be doers of the word and not hearers only.

JAMES 1:22 HCSB

It's important to listen closely to the stories we hear in church. But don't stop there. The next step is to do what the Bible says!

We know from the Bible that God is happy when His people help the poor, act kindly, and tell others about His love. You can show your faith in God by doing the things He asks, and others will feel God's love through you! So the next time you hear a Bible story, try to figure out what God might be asking you to do. Then go do it!

THOUGHT OF THE DAY

Think of your favorite Bible story. What lesson can you put into action today?

PRAY TODAY

Dear God, thank You for giving me the Bible to teach me how to live. Help me to be a doer of Your Word! Amen.

BE AN ENCOURAGER

You must encourage one another each day.

HEBREWS 3:13 CEV

You can do it!" "I'm on your side." "Don't give up." These are all simple things you can say to encourage someone.

How do you feel when you're trying something for the first time or when you're doing something that is hard work? Isn't it easier to keep on trying if someone gives you encouragement? The Bible reminds us that we should encourage one another each day. So today, look around and see who needs to hear some encouraging words. Then think of something to say that will help them!

THOUGHT OF THE DAY

What can you say or do today to encourage the people you know?

PRAY TODAY

Dear God, please help me share words of encouragement with my family and friends. Amen.

GOD HOLDS YOUR HAND

"Don't be afraid, for I am with you. Don't be discouraged, for I am your God. I will strengthen you and help you. I will hold you up with my victorious right hand."

ISAIAH 41:10 NLT

Have you ever been afraid to do something? Maybe you had to walk into a new school or class. Or maybe you had to try something you'd never done before. If you are afraid, isn't it great to have someone go with you and hold your hand?

God says that He wants to help you whenever you feel afraid. Even though you can't see Him, He is always there, just like a best friend. You can imagine God holding your hand in His and walking with you when you're afraid. He will give you strength and courage because He loves you!

THOUGHT OF THE DAY

There's nothing to fear when you know God is near!

PRAY TODAY

Dear God, thank You for always holding my hand and helping me be strong and brave. Amen.

JESUS WILL ALWAYS LOVE YOU

"As the Father has loved Me, I have also loved you. Remain in My love."

JOHN 15:9 HCSB

The Bible makes this promise: Jesus loves you. No matter who you are. No matter how you feel. No matter what you do. Jesus loves you.

Long ago, Jesus showed His love for you by leaving heaven to come to live on earth. Jesus helped and healed people to show the power of His love. He taught His friends about God, and they wrote His words in the Bible so you can read them today! Long before you were born, Jesus loved you. And Jesus will never stop loving you.

THOUGHT OF THE DAY

Do you know someone who might need to know about Jesus' love? Share it with them today!

PRAY TODAY

Dear God, thank You for always loving me. Help me share Your love with others. Amen.

BEING COURTEOUS

. . . to speak evil of no one, to avoid quarreling, to be gentle, and to show perfect courtesy toward all people.

TITUS 3:2 ESV

Being courteous means using good manners and showing kindness to others. There are many ways to show courtesy at home and at school. Using words like "please" and "thank you" and saying "I'm sorry" or "excuse me" are all ways to be courteous and kind. You can also listen patiently when others are talking and take turns when you're playing. These words and actions help us all get along together. They are ways to show we care about other people like God wants us to. Look for ways to be courteous today!

THOUGHT OF THE DAY

Saying "thanks" and "please" will help to put a friend at ease.

PRAY TODAY

Dear God, please help me to always treat others with courtesy and kindness. Amen.

POWERFUL WORDS

Lord, help me control my tongue; help me be careful about what I say.

PSALM 141:3 NCV

Have you ever noticed that words have power? Hurtful words can make people sad or angry. But kind and helpful words can make someone feel loved or even help them smile.

The Bible says that we need to be careful about the words we say. Sometimes when we're angry, we might say words that hurt someone's feelings. When that happens, we need to use kind words and ask for forgiveness. You can ask God to help you think before you speak. Remember that all of your words are powerful!

THOUGHT OF THE DAY

Every day we get to choose the kinds of words we want to use.

PRAY TODAY

Dear God, please help me remember that my words are important. Let me use my words to help others. Amen.

LEARN FROM GOD

Listen carefully to wisdom; set your mind on under-standing.

PROVERBS 2:2 NCV

God wants you to make good choices. In order to do that, you have to listen to wisdom. And the best place to find wisdom is God!

God knows everything, and He loves everyone. You can read God's Word to learn about His wisdom. The Bible is full of good advice and great stories that show us how to live. You can also talk with God and ask Him to lead you every day. As you spend time with God and learn more about Him, you'll get to know what His wisdom looks like. Then you can make wise choices too!

THOUGHT OF THE DAY

God wants to share His wisdom with you! All you have to do is ask.

PRAY TODAY

Dear God, I want to make wise choices. Please share Your wisdom with me! Amen.

YOU CAN TRUST GOD

So we will not be afraid even if the earth shakes, or the mountains fall into the sea.

PSALM 46:2 NCV

D o you ever feel afraid? Sometimes scary things can happen, but all you have to do is remember that God is always with you. And God will always take care of you!

God is bigger than anything you might be afraid of. If you don't like noisy storms, the next time you hear thunder, say a little prayer to God, and thank Him for taking care of you. If you're afraid of the dark, remember that God is with you. No matter what, you can always trust that God is watching over you.

THOUGHT OF THE DAY

The best way to beat fear is with faith. Don't let fear win!

PRAY TODAY

Dear God, when I am feeling afraid, I will remember that You said to "fear not." Thank You for giving me peace and courage. Amen.

GOOD DEEDS AND GOOD HEARTS

"A good person produces good deeds from a good heart."

LUKE 6:45 NLT

When you do something kind for someone, it is called a *good deed*. And the Bible says that when we do good deeds for others, we show that we have a good heart!

There are lots of ways to do good deeds for the people you know. You can draw a picture or make a card for a neighbor. You can help your parents or grand-parents by doing your chores with a smile. You can share your toys and take turns at the playground. You can help someone who needs a friend. What are some other good deeds that will show your good heart?

THOUGHT OF THE DAY

When someone looks like they're in need, that's the time to do good deeds!

PRAY TODAY

Dear God, when my family and friends need help, please help me to be kind and do what I can. Amen.

EVERYONE DESERVES KINDNESS

"Don't criticize, and then you won't be criticized."

MATTHEW 7:1 TLB

D o you like it when people are nice to you? Of course! It feels great when someone gives you a compliment or invites you to play. Everyone wants to be treated kindly.

But it can be tempting to say unkind words. Especially when someone acts, dresses, or speaks differently from you. Be careful! When you criticize others, it's like you're saying you are perfect and they've got it wrong. But only God is perfect! It's better to show kindness to everyone. We don't all do things the same way, but that's just fine. Everyone is unique, and everyone is important to God!

THOUGHT OF THE DAY

Even if everyone around you is speaking unkind words, you can choose kind ones!

PRAY TODAY

Dear God, thank You for loving everyone. Help me remember that everyone should be treated kindly! Amen.

THREE KEYS

Rejoice always, pray continually, give thanks in all circumstances; for this is God's will for you in Christ Jesus.

1 Thessalonians 5:16-18 NIV

D o you ever wonder what God wants you to do? Well, here's some good news: there are three simple keys to pleasing God. And today's verse tells you what they are!

First, always rejoice. That means be on the lookout for things to be glad about. Second, always pray. Praying is just talking to God, and you can do that wherever you are! Third, always give thanks. There are so many things to be thankful for! If you rejoice, pray, and give thanks every day, you can know you are doing just what God wants you to do!

THOUGHT OF THE DAY

Name some things you can rejoice about, pray about, and thank God for today!

PRAY TODAY

Dear God, I love You, and I want to please You. Help me remember to rejoice, pray, and give thanks every day. Amen.

BEING PATIENT

Always be humble and gentle. Be patient and accept each other with love.

EPHESIANS 4:2 ICB

Sometimes it is hard to wait for someone who is slower than you. Other times it is hard to understand why someone can't do something that is easy for you to do.

Being patient means being willing to slow down and help someone else, even if you are in a hurry. It means being willing to explain something more than once so that another person can learn how to do it. Loving others means taking the time to be patient. Jesus is always patient with us, so we should try to be patient with others!

THOUGHT OF THE DAY

When was a time someone showed love for you by being patient?

PRAY TODAY

Dear God, please help me to be patient with other people, just as You are patient with me. Amen.

WINNING WITH GOD

"So you want first place? Then take the last place. Be the servant of all."

MARK 9:35 MSG

To God, winning doesn't look like crossing the finish line before everyone else or getting first place in a contest. God is most interested in how we love and care for each other. So you actually win first place with God by putting yourself last! Let someone else go before you in line. Spend your allowance on something you think would cheer up a friend. Take extra time teaching a younger sibling how to play a new game. You might not get a big prize, but you will be a winner in God's eyes!

THOUGHT OF THE DAY

How can you put someone else first today?

PRAY TODAY

Dear God, sometimes I really like to be first. But help me learn to put myself last so that I can win with You! Amen.

WHAT A FRIEND!

"As the Father has loved Me, I have also loved You. Remain in My love."

JOHN 15:9 HCSB

What makes a good friendship great? Spending time together! When you spend time with your friends, you get to know each other really well, and you learn to depend on each other.

Jesus is the very best friend you could ever have. So be sure to spend lots of time with Him! He loves to listen to your ideas, hear about your day, and help you through hard times. He cares about everything that matters to you. And nothing makes Him happier than sharing His love with you. So make time to hang out with Jesus today! He's a friend you can really count on.

THOUGHT OF THE DAY
Pick a time every day to talk with Jesus!

PRAY TODAY
Dear Jesus, thank You for being my very best friend! I want to spend time with You and get to know You better. Amen.

GOD'S LOVE LASTS

You are my God, and I will thank you. You are my God, and I will praise your greatness. Thank the Lord because he is good. His love continues forever.

PSALM 118:28–29 ICB

D o you have a toy that runs on batteries? What happens when the batteries die? Your toy stops working. Maybe you have a favorite shirt or pair of shoes. What happens if you wear them all the time? They wear out!

There's one thing you have that never stops. It doesn't even need batteries! Do you know what it is? God's love! The Bible reminds us that God's love lasts forever. It never wears out, and you can't ever use it all up. There will always be plenty of God's love.

THOUGHT OF THE DAY

Nothing is greater than God's love!

PRAY TODAY

Dear God, thank You for loving me forever. I'm so glad there is always more than enough of Your love! Amen.

ACTS OF LOVE

There are three things that remain—faith, hope, and love—and the greatest of these is love.

1 CORINTHIANS 13:13 TLB

Sometimes we think of love as a feeling, but the Bible says love is an action—something we do. That means we can act in loving ways even when we may not feel like it.

How can you act in loving ways? You can wait when you'd rather rush. You can always choose to say kind words. Don't brag or act like you are better than others, and say you're sorry when you're wrong. And it's always loving to tell the truth, even if it's hard to do. Love isn't always easy, but the Bible says it's the greatest way to live!

THOUGHT OF THE DAY

What are some things you can do to show your love to others?

PRAY TODAY

Dear God, thank You for loving me. Please help me to act in ways that show Your love to others. Amen.

GOD BRINGS JOY

But let all those rejoice who put their trust in You; Let them ever shout for joy, because You defend them; Let those also who love Your name Be joyful in You.

PSALM 5:11 NKJV

The Bible is filled with stories about people with big problems. Abraham had to move away from all his friends. Moses was chased by thousands of soldiers. Queen Esther faced a scheming Haman. David fought a giant. But do you know what all these people had in common? They trusted God, and He took care of them when they went through hard times. Because of God's love, they were each able to rejoice even when bad things happened! Joy comes from knowing that no matter what happens, God loves you and is always with you.

THOUGHT OF THE DAY

God's love for every girl and boy can turn your troubles into joy!

PRAY TODAY

Dear God, help me remember to trust You whenever I am scared or have a problem. Amen.

BE KIND TO EVERYBODY

Be kind to one another, tenderhearted, forgiving one another, as God in Christ forgave you.

EPHESIANS 4:32 ESV

God is very clear: He wants you to treat everyone with kindness. But what if someone isn't kind to you? The rules don't change! That's because God loves each of us equally, no matter how we act.

The good news is, God can help you choose kindness. If someone says or does something unkind, try to stay calm. You can always decide to walk away or say something nice instead. Ask God to help you be patient and forgive quickly. He will bless you when you try to be kind!

THOUGHT OF THE DAY

Sometimes people aren't kind because no one has shown them how to be. Show someone kindness today!

PRAY TODAY

Dear God, please help me to be kind and patient with everyone, even when it's hard. Amen.

GETTING TO KNOW HIM

Yes, it is through Christ we all have the right to come to the Father in one Spirit.

EPHESIANS 2:18 NCV

Have you ever wondered what God is really like? Here's a clue: look at Jesus! The Bible says Jesus is the key to understanding who God is.

Think about your favorite stories of Jesus. How does He treat people? What does He care about? Those are the things that are important to God. Jesus loves people unconditionally—that means "no matter what." That's how God loves each of us. So invite Jesus to live in your heart today. When you get to know Jesus, you get to know God!

THOUGHT OF THE DAY
What's your favorite story about Jesus?

PRAY TODAY
Dear God, thank You for sending Jesus so I can understand You better! Amen.

HEARING GOD

"He who has ears to hear, let him hear."

MATTHEW 11:15 ESV

Stop and listen. What do you hear? Birds singing? People talking? Music playing? The Bible says that if we have ears, we should listen closely so we can hear God!

What do you think God's voice sounds like? It might sound like someone reading the Bible to you or telling you Bible stories at church. Maybe it sounds like your family praying. Sometimes we hear God's voice inside of us, reminding us to be kind, to do the right thing, or just to be still. Listen closely. What is God saying to you?

THOUGHT OF THE DAY

Pay attention today and see if you can hear God telling you things!

PRAY TODAY

Dear God, thank You for giving me ears to hear. Help me always listen for Your voice speaking to my heart! Amen.

GIVING IS BEST!

"It is more blessed to give than to receive."

ACTS 20:35 HCSB

Think of a time you gave someone a gift they really loved. Were you excited as they were opening it? Didn't you love seeing the smile on their face? It's fun to get presents, but it can feel even better to give them!

You don't even have to wait for Christmas or a birthday to give gifts. There are always people who need clothes, books, or food. Do you have some nice things you just don't use very much? Ask your parents about ways to donate them to people in need. Your gifts might be exactly what someone else was hoping for! How cool is that?

THOUGHT OF THE DAY

Getting presents sure is fun. Giving them helps everyone!

PRAY TODAY

Dear God, please help me give joyfully to others all through the year. It's so much fun! Amen.

WHAT'S IN YOUR FUTURE?

We can make our plans, but the Lord determines our steps.

PROVERBS 16:9 NLT

Is there something you want to do when you grow up? Isn't it fun to have dreams? God has a dream for your future too! And He wants to help you make it come true.

God's dreams and your dreams might be the same, or they might not. If things don't go exactly the way you expect, don't worry! Remember that God is taking care of you and His plans are very good.

No one knows what the future will bring. Keep dreaming along with God, and see where He takes you!

THOUGHT OF THE DAY

Trust God with your present, and He will make your future bright.

PRAY TODAY

Dear God, thank You for planning so many good things for my future! Help me trust You with all my dreams. Amen.

PRAY ABOUT IT!

"The eyes of the LORD watch over those who do right, and his hears are open to their prayers."

1 PETER 3:12 NLT

Did you know that you have a secret tool you can use any time, day or night? Prayer! You can pray about anything any time you want. Do you want to get better at something? Pray for God's help. Is something bothering you? Pray for God's comfort. Are you nervous about meeting someone new? Pray for God's peace. Anything you want to pray about, God is ready to listen. He loves for you to share your heart with Him, and He can always help you. So don't waste time worrying about anything. Pray right away!

THOUGHT OF THE DAY
Prayer changes things. Try it and see!

PRAY TODAY
Dear God, thank You for always being there to listen when I pray. Help me remember to talk to You when I'm worried. Amen.

HOW TO PRAY

"So when you pray, you should pray like this: 'Our Father in heaven, we pray that your name will always be kept holy. We pray that your kingdom will come. We pray that what you want will be done, here on earth as it is in heaven.'"

MATTHEW 6:9–10 ICB

Do you ever wonder how to pray? One day, Jesus' friends asked Him how they should pray, so Jesus taught them a prayer we call "The Lord's Prayer." You can follow the same pattern that Jesus taught!

Begin by thanking and praising God. Ask God to make His plans here in the world happen the way they should. Then tell God what you need. Next, ask God for His forgiveness for the things you have done that are wrong. Finally, ask God to help you act the way He wants you to.

Jesus wants us to pray always. And He promises that He'll always listen!

THOUGHT OF THE DAY

I'm so glad that every day I can come to God and pray.

PRAY TODAY

Dear God, thank You for always listening to me when I pray. Help me hear what You have to say to me too. Amen.

YOUR VERY BEST FRIEND

Jesus Christ is the same yesterday and today and forever.

HEBREWS 13:8 ESV

Do you have some really good friends? Good friends are people you can count on to do what they say. And they always take care of each other!

When you ask Jesus to come live in your heart, He becomes your best friend. You can tell Him whatever you're thinking about, and He promises to care for you and help you. If you make a wrong choice or a big mistake, you never have to worry! Jesus will always love and forgive you. In fact, with Jesus, you not only get a best friend— you get a forever friend!

THOUGHT OF THE DAY

Who are some of your good friends? How do you show each other you care?

PRAY TODAY

Dear Jesus, thank You for being my very best friend! I'm so glad we're friends forever. Amen.

STAY IN CONTROL

Don't let your spirit rush to be angry, for anger abides in the heart of fools.

ECCLESIASTES 7:9 HCSB

There is nothing wrong with feeling angry. But when we let that anger control how we act, we can make foolish choices that hurt other people.

God tells us not to get angry quickly. And He can help! When you feel yourself getting mad, stop and pray that God will help you stay in control. You can also take deep breaths or count slowly to ten. Once you've taken a little time, you'll be able to speak and act more kindly. Kind words will help the situation get better much faster than angry words!

THOUGHT OF THE DAY
Be slow to get angry and quick to be kind!

PRAY TODAY
Dear God, it's not always easy to control my angry feelings, but I know that You will help me! Amen.

LOOKING AT THE HEART

"God does not see the same way people see. People look at the outside of a person, but the LORD looks at the heart."

1 SAMUEL 16:7 NCV

It's tempting to spend a lot of time thinking about what we look like. Sometimes it can seem like people only care about appearances. But that's not how God works! God sees who you are inside, and He loves every part of you.

Sometimes it's good to look your very best. But what you care about and how you treat people is much more important than what you look like. Don't let your outside appearance affect how you think about yourself. Your heart is what matters to God, and He thinks you are beautiful!

THOUGHT OF THE DAY

What are some things you like about yourself?

PRAY TODAY

Dear God, thank You for looking at my heart. Help me to see others and myself like You do! Amen.

WORSHIPPING GOD

Oh come, let us worship and bow down; let us kneel before the LORD, our Maker!

PSALM 95:6 ESV

The Bible tells us to worship God because He is the One who made us. He is a mighty King!

There are many ways we can show that we love and respect God. We can kneel or bow our heads when we pray. We can sing and raise our hands to Him in joy and thanks! We can obey His words in the Bible. Just think about how amazing God is and about all the wonderful things He has made! He totally deserves all of our praise and worship. So raise your voice or bow your head or start dancing! God is great!

THOUGHT OF THE DAY

How do you want to worship God today?

PRAY TODAY

Dear God, You are greater than anything I can understand. Today I will choose to worship and praise You. Amen.

MAD WORDS OR GENTLE WORDS

A gentle answer will calm a person's anger, but an unkind answer will cause more anger.

PROVERBS 15:1 NCV

Sometimes when we feel angry, we say mad words. Then, when other people hear our mad words, they get mad too. Pretty soon, everyone is yelling at each other! Mad words just make anger bigger. But there's another way!

The Bible says that gentle words are best. They can actually stop anger! Gentle words might sound like "I'm not happy right now" or "we need to just calm down." We can also say "I'm sorry" if we've done something to make another person angry. Mad words just make things worse, but gentle words can make things better!

THOUGHT OF THE DAY

Gentle words are strong enough to stop anger.

PRAY TODAY

Dear God, You know I get angry sometimes. Please help me not to say mad words and, instead, speak words that are gentle. Amen.

HOW TO BE A GOOD FRIEND

My dear, dear friends, if God loved us like this, we certainly ought to love each other.

1 JOHN 4:11 MSG

God wants us to love our friends just like He loves us. That's a pretty strong love! What do you think that would look like?

God listens to our prayers, so we should listen when our friends share stories or ask for help. God cares for us, so we should take care of our friends and show them love. And most importantly, God always works for our good. So look for ways to build your friends up! When you do these things, you'll become better friends with everyone—including God!

THOUGHT OF THE DAY

God rejoices over us, so we should rejoice over each other! Thank God for your friends today.

PRAY TODAY

Dear God, thank You for my friends! We all have so much fun. Help me to be the very best friend I can be. Amen.

NO ONE LIKE YOU!

You made all the delicate, inner parts of my body and knit me together in my mother's womb.

PSALM 139:13 NLT

When God made you, He did everything right. He created you in His image with love and care, and He made only one of you. There is no one else in the world exactly like you! What a treasure you are!

You may be tempted to compare yourself to other people, but there's no point. You're unique! No one else has your story or your gifts. Your smile and your laugh make your face light up like no one else's. Trust God's work and know that you are marvelous, just the way God made you.

THOUGHT OF THE DAY

God made you special! What are some special things about you?

PRAY TODAY

Dear God, thank You for making me the way I am! Please stop me from comparing myself to anyone. Amen.

A LIGHT OF KINDNESS

Let everyone see that you are gentle and kind. The Lord is coming soon.

PHILIPPIANS 4:5 NCV

Before Jesus went up to heaven, He told us He'd come back someday. What a great day that will be! Everyone will see how good Jesus is, and His goodness will make the whole world bright.

Until then, God wants us to shine brightly for Him. You can do that by showing kindness to each person you meet! When you are kind to others, they learn that God thinks they are important and loved. And everyone needs to know God's love! So always choose kindness. You will brighten so many lives.

THOUGHT OF THE DAY

Kindness is like a candle—it gives warmth and light!

PRAY TODAY

Dear God, help me find ways to show kindness every day. I want to be Your light! Amen.

WHO IS YOUR NEIGHBOR?

Yes indeed, it is good when you truly obey our Lord's command, "You must love and help your neighbors just as much as you love and take care of yourself."

JAMES 2:8 TLB

The Bible says to love your neighbor. But does that mean you should love only the people who live in your neighborhood? No way!

A neighbor is anyone God brings into your life. It could be the person who lives down the street *and* a kid across the world who needs help! Neighbors can be old or young, friends or strangers. They can be people you really like or even those you don't like very much. God asks us to love each person the same way you love yourself. How do you do that? You can start by praying for them!

THOUGHT OF THE DAY

What are three ways you can love a "neighbor" today?

PRAY TODAY

Dear God, it's fun to think of the whole world as a neighborhood. Please help me show Your love to all my neighbors! Amen.

FAMILY HARMONY

And above all these put on love, which binds everything together in perfect harmony.

COLOSSIANS 3:14 ESV

Have you ever heard a band play music? The different instruments each look and sound different. A tuba is big and makes a low sound. A flute is long and thin and makes high notes. The drums say "boom, boom, boom" or "rat-a-tat-tat." But when they all play together they make wonderful music. That's called harmony.

In a family, each person has different feelings and does different things. But when everyone in a family works together with love, they live together in perfect harmony, just like an awesome band! And that's exactly how God wants us to live.

THOUGHT OF THE DAY

What part do you play in your family?

PRAY TODAY

Dear God, thank You for my family. We are not all the same, so we need Your love to help us make beautiful harmony together. Amen.

GOD'S GOOD PROMISES

Surely goodness and mercy shall follow me all the days of my life, and I shall dwell in the house of the Lord forever.

PSALM 23:6 ESV

The Bible is filled with wonderful promises. In the verse above, David reminds us of God's promise that goodness and mercy will be with us every day and that we will live with God forever! God never breaks His promises. That means that even if we do not feel like good things are happening, we can be sure that God is still good. Why not practice looking for something good every single day? When things aren't going the way you like, think about how God is with you even then. God is good, and His promises are always true!

THOUGHT OF THE DAY

Can you think of at least three good things about today?

PRAY TODAY

Dear God, thank You for Your good promises to me and to my family. I love You. Amen.

GOD'S HELPING HANDS

Now the God of all grace, who called you to His eternal glory in Christ Jesus, will personally restore, establish, strengthen, and support you.

1 PETER 5:10 HCSB

God is the greatest Helper there is. No matter what problem you're facing, God will guide you through. When things get tough, God is stronger. When you feel sad, God will comfort you. And when you feel happy, God will celebrate with you!

God's love never ends, and neither does His help. He never gets tired or distracted. Your life is His greatest joy, and He loves to share it with you! He is all around you, all the time. So take His hand and follow His lead. He's here to help.

THOUGHT OF THE DAY
Trust God and watch what He can do!

PRAY TODAY
Dear God, thank You for Your always-there, never-failing helping hands! I love knowing I can count on You. Amen.

FAMILY HARMONY

And above all these put on love, which binds everything together in perfect harmony.

COLOSSIANS 3:14 ESV

Have you ever heard a band play music? The different instruments each look and sound different. A tuba is big and makes a low sound. A flute is long and thin and makes high notes. The drums say "boom, boom, boom" or "rat-a-tat-tat." But when they all play together they make wonderful music. That's called harmony.

In a family, each person has different feelings and does different things. But when everyone in a family works together with love, they live together in perfect harmony, just like an awesome band! And that's exactly how God wants us to live.

THOUGHT OF THE DAY

What part do you play in your family?

PRAY TODAY

Dear God, thank You for my family. We are not all the same, so we need Your love to help us make beautiful harmony together. Amen.

SOMETHING GOOD

And we know that for those who love God all things work together for good, for those who are called according to his purpose.

ROMANS 8:28 ESV

Have you ever made a mistake when drawing a picture? Did you ever build something and then it broke? Sometimes when we make mistakes or ruin something, we just toss it out. But God says even when we make mistakes or feel like we have done something wrong He will never give up on us! He will always love us. God can even take our mistakes and make something good out of them. He will never give up on us, and He loves to surprise us with blessings. What a wonderful God!

THOUGHT OF THE DAY

Look for ways God is making something good in your life today!

PRAY TODAY

Dear God, I don't understand why things go wrong sometimes, but I am so glad You can make anything into something good. Amen.

PRAISE EVERY DAY!

I will always thank the Lord; I will never stop praising him.

PSALM 34:1 GNT

God is so good. He gives us strength and courage. He helps us feel joyful when we're sad. He has blessed us with families and good friends. He loves us all the time. So it makes sense that we should praise Him all the time!

Praise means celebrating how good God is. You can praise God by singing songs about Him, making up a dance for Him, or simply telling Him how much you love Him. You can praise Him out loud or silently in your heart. However you praise God, remember you can praise Him all day long!

THOUGHT OF THE DAY

Remember to praise God every time you pray.

PRAY TODAY

Dear God, You are amazing! Help me remember to praise You every single day. Amen.

GOD'S HOUSE

"Be glad and rejoice, because your reward is great in heaven."

MATTHEW 5:12A HCSB

D o you love to invite friends over to your house? Isn't it fun to share what we have with the people we like? Jesus sure thinks so. That's why He wants us all to come over to His house: heaven! In fact, when you invite Jesus into your heart, He invites *you* to live with Him in heaven forever.

No one knows exactly what heaven will be like. But the Bible does tell us that there will be no more sadness or sickness, and you'll get to meet Jesus face to face. What a wonderful place to call home!

THOUGHT OF THE DAY

When you meet Jesus, what do you think you'll say to Him?

PRAY TODAY

Dear God, thank You for preparing such a wonderful forever home for me in heaven! Amen.

HOW TO LOVE GOD

This is love for God: to keep his commands.

1 JOHN 5:3 NIV

One of the best ways to tell your parents you love them is to obey them. When you do what your mom and dad ask, it shows them that you trust and respect them.

God feels the same way when you obey His commands. When He tells you what to do, it's because He cares for you. If you obey Him, you're showing that you love Him too, and you believe that He knows what's best for you. How can you obey God today?

THOUGHT OF THE DAY

How do you think God feels when you obey Him?

PRAY TODAY

Dear God, help me choose to obey You so I can show You how much I love You. Amen.

YOU MAKE A DIFFERENCE

"For the Son of Man is going to come with His angels in the glory of His Father, and then He will reward each according to what he has done."

MATTHEW 16:27 HCSB

Think of a time someone made you feel great. Did a friend tell you a funny story to cheer you up? Did your mom give you a hug? Even small things can make a big difference!

The world is full of people who need help. Every day you can make someone's day brighter in small ways. When you say kind things or invite someone new to play with you, you are changing that person's day for the better. You never know who might need exactly what you give them!

THOUGHT OF THE DAY

Something as small as a smile can do big things!

PRAY TODAY

Dear God, please show me how I can make a difference to someone today. Amen.

WILLING TO FORGIVE

Make allowance for each other's faults, and forgive anyone who offends you. Remember, the Lord forgave you, so you must forgive others.

COLOSSIANS 3:13 NLT

Doesn't it feel great to know that God forgives you, no matter what? What a great gift!

Because forgiveness is so wonderful, God also wants us to forgive each other. That's not always easy—especially if your feelings still hurt or you're still angry. But God can help you. If you're having a hard time forgiving, think about a time you made a mistake. Then remember how God forgave you! Ask Him to make you willing to forgive. If you're ready to try, God is ready to help you.

THOUGHT OF THE DAY

If there's someone you need to forgive, talk things over with your parents too. They'd love to help!

PRAY TODAY

Dear God, please help me remember Your love and forgiveness when I need to forgive someone else. Amen.

PRAY FOR OUR LEADERS

Pray for kings and others in power, so that we may live quiet and peaceful lives as we worship and honor God.

1 TIMOTHY 2:2 CEV

Sometimes we think that leaders have everything figured out. But everybody needs God's help and guidance. Especially people who are in charge!

God can help your teachers know how best to reach every single student. He shows your pastor how to preach wise, hopeful words in church and support the people in your congregation. He can guide leaders in your community to make good decisions. Even the president needs God's wisdom!

Leaders can help people grow and feel God's peace. They have a big responsibility. And you can make a big difference by praying for them!

THOUGHT OF THE DAY

You don't have to know someone to pray for them. Who would you like to pray for today?

PRAY TODAY

Dear God, thanks that You watch over all of us. Please help our leaders make good decisions so everyone can live happily and peacefully. Amen.

LOVING PATIENCE

Love is patient and kind.

1 CORINTHIANS 13:4A ESV

Has someone ever told you to be patient? Being patient doesn't just mean waiting. It means waiting *peacefully* and trusting that you will get what you need at the right time.

When you're patient around your parents, you show that you believe they love you and will take care of you. When you're patient with your friends, you show that you care about them and their ideas. And when you're patient with God, you show that you love Him and trust Him to care for you. Patience isn't always easy, but it's a great way to show love!

THOUGHT OF THE DAY

Patience comes with practice. Find two ways to practice patience today!

PRAY TODAY

Dear God, I know You want what's best for me. Help me to be patient with You and with my friends and family. Amen.

SURPRISE!

The LORD your God is God of all gods and Lord of all lords. He is the great God, who is strong and wonderful.

DEUTERONOMY 10:17 NCV

God loves to surprise us! You can see it all through the Bible. Hannah and Abraham thought they were too old to have children, but God gave them a son. Gideon had only a few soldiers holding torches and horns, but God helped him defeat a huge army.

Stories like this show us God's strength and power. Doesn't that make you confident that God can help you too? That's why it's important to read Bible stories! We might not see a solution, but God can do anything. So let God surprise you with what He can do for you!

THOUGHT OF THE DAY

Can you think of a time when God surprised you?

PRAY TODAY

Dear God, thank You that nothing is impossible for You! I can't wait to see how You will surprise me next. Amen.

KEEP ON TRYING

We can rejoice, too, when we run into problems and trials, for we know that they are good for us—they help us learn to be patient. And patience develops strength of character in us and helps us trust God more each time we use it until finally our hope and faith are strong and steady.

ROMANS 5:3-4 TLB

Sometimes when things are hard to do, we might feel like giving up. But if we quit, we won't learn how to do them. If you gave up trying whenever things were hard to do, you might never learn to do important things like write your name or count or ride your bike or make friends. The Bible says it is good to keep trying when things are hard because that helps us grow. Remember, you're not in this alone. God will always help us learn new things if we don't give up!

THOUGHT OF THE DAY

Trying hard is the thing to do when you're learning something new!

PRAY TODAY

Dear God, thank You for helping me to grow. Please help me to keep trying even when things are hard to do. Amen.

GOD-TIME

I . . . wait quietly before God, for my hope is in him.

PSALM 62:5 NLT

Have you noticed how every day has lots of different times? There's morning time, bedtime, lunchtime, dinnertime, homework time, playtime, screen time, and nighttime. But have you ever heard of "God-time"? You can talk to God, praise Him, and thank Him all through the day; but it is also important to set aside some special, quiet time each day just to spend with God. Maybe that's what you're doing right now, when you're reading this book! Taking time for God each day will make all your other times even better!

THOUGHT OF THE DAY

When will you take some special time to be quiet with God today?

PRAY TODAY

Dear God, I want to know You better. Please help me remember to take time to talk and listen to You today. Amen.

GOD WILL LEAD THE WAY

During the day the L<small>ORD</small> went ahead of his people in a thick cloud, and during the night he went ahead of them in a flaming fire.

E<small>XODUS</small> 13:21 C<small>EV</small>

God told Moses to lead the people of Israel out of Egypt. But He didn't give Moses directions once they got out! Instead, God appeared in front of them as a huge cloud every day and as fire every night. All they had to do was follow God!

God wants you to follow Him every day too. But you don't need Him to be a cloud or a fireball. Read your Bible each day to learn about His ways. Spend time with God in prayers, and ask Him to show you what to do. If you look for God, He will lead you to wonderful things!

THOUGHT OF THE DAY

The Bible is like a treasure map—it will lead you to God's great plans!

PRAY TODAY

Dear God, thank You for Your good plans for me. Please lead me and help me find the right way to go! Amen.

ANYTHING IS POSSIBLE!

Jesus said to him . . . "Everything is possible to the one who believes."

MARK 9:23 HCSB

Have you ever wanted to do something hard? Maybe you're learning something new—like playing a sport or an instrument. Maybe you're trying to make friends at a new school. God has good news for you. He can help you do anything!

God loves to help His children do great things. So ask for His help! It may be hard work, but you won't be doing it alone. Anytime you feel frustrated, ask Him to give you strength. If you feel nervous, ask for His peace. God is on your side. He will never let you down.

THOUGHT OF THE DAY
What can God help you do today?

PRAY TODAY
Dear God, I'm so happy that nothing is too hard for You! Please help me work hard and remember that You are always with me. Amen.

WALK IN TRUTH

I have no greater joy than this: to hear that my children are walking in the truth.

3 JOHN 1:4 HCSB

You probably know what it means to tell the truth. But what does God mean when He says we should *walk* in the truth?

He means that we should choose His ways all the time. So as you walk around today, look for ways you can follow God's direction. Treat people with His love and kindness. Help those who need it. Notice good things around you and thank God for them. Share God's love with your friends! When you walk through your day with God, you'll be sure to walk in the truth.

THOUGHT OF THE DAY

Walk with God and choose His way; He will guide you every day!

PRAY TODAY

Dear God, help me remember to walk with You all day so I can always walk in the truth. Amen.

KEEP IT UP!

So let's not get tired of doing what is good. At just the right time we will reap a harvest of blessing if we don't give up.

GALATIANS 6:9 NLT

Treating others with kindness, love, and generosity is always best. But it can be hard sometimes. Especially if you don't feel like anyone is really paying attention. Don't give up! What you do matters to God, and He loves that you are following His ways. The Bible says we should never get tired of doing good. Maybe you can't tell if your actions are making a difference, but keep it up! God is doing great things through you. And He promises that one day, in His perfect timing, you'll be rewarded too!

THOUGHT OF THE DAY

Keep on striving to do good, just like Jesus said we should!

PRAY TODAY

Dear God, please give me strength and patience to keep doing the things You want me to do! Amen.

GOD CAN USE YOU

Every good gift and every perfect gift is from above, coming down from the Father of lights.

JAMES 1:17 NKJV

Every good gift in your life is from God! That means your family, your friends, your home, your stuff, your talents, your favorite things to do, and even your favorite birthday present are all blessings sent to you from your heavenly Father.

God wants you to share your blessings with others. For example, you can share your toys, take time to help someone learn to tie his or her shoes, or help clean up a mess. Sometimes when you do something nice or share something God has given you, it feels so good that the act of sharing can be a gift of its own!

THOUGHT OF THE DAY
Helping other people can feel so good!

PRAY TODAY
Dear God, thank You for all of the good gifts You have given me. I want You to use me to help others too. Amen.

HOW TO GET FAITH

So faith comes from hearing, and hearing through the word of Christ.

ROMANS 10:17 ESV

If you want to buy something, you can order it online or buy it in a store. But how do you get faith?

The Bible says that if we want to have faith, we need to listen to what God tells us—in the Bible! When we hear stories about Bible heroes and about Jesus' life, we learn how God loves and helps His people. We also learn about the promises God makes to help us and love us. We can trust the words in the Bible because they are true. And when we know the truth about God, our faith grows and grows!

THOUGHT OF THE DAY

God's Word makes faith grow.

PRAY TODAY

Dear God, thank You for giving us the Bible. Help my faith to grow as I listen to Your words and get to know You better. Amen.

ALWAYS PEACEFUL

Now may the Lord of peace himself give you peace at all times in every way. The Lord be with you all.

2 Thessalonians 3:16 esv

Feeling peaceful means you feel calm and certain that everything is OK. What a great way to feel! And the Bible says with God, we can feel peaceful all the time. God gives us peace through His great big love. It's a love that sticks around in good times and hard times. And like His love, God never changes! He is always strong, always powerful, and He always keeps His promises. So if you ever feel sad or scared or angry, remember God. He is right here, waiting to give you His wonderful peace!

THOUGHT OF THE DAY

Every day is different, but God is always the same!

PRAY TODAY

Dear God, when I feel worried or angry or sad, please help me remember Your love. Help me feel peaceful every day. Amen.

STRONG BODIES

You were bought by God for a price. So honor God with your bodies.

1 CORINTHIANS 6:20 NCV

God wants you to take good care of your body so that you can do all the wonderful things He has planned for you! Two important things you can do to be healthy and strong are eating good food and getting enough sleep. But something else you can do is move your body! Running, jumping, playing games, swimming, and dancing are some great ways to keep your body moving and healthy. Try different kinds of things until you find something you really enjoy. Then you will have fun while you build a strong body!

THOUGHT OF THE DAY

What kinds of activities do you enjoy to help your body be strong? What's something new you could try?

PRAY TODAY

Dear God, I want to take good care of my body so I can honor You. Help me make healthy choices today. Amen.

GOOD RULES

Practice God's law—get a reputation for wisdom.

PROVERBS 28:7 MSG

God made you to be a special part of His world. And He gives us all good rules to follow so we can live the life He wants us to have.

Following God's rules takes practice. Just like you have to play a game several times before you can do it well, you can work on God's rules every day. Don't worry if you make a mistake! Just decide what you want to do differently, and try that next time. Pretty soon, you'll be in the good habit of following good rules!

THOUGHT OF THE DAY

Before you speak or act, ask yourself, "Will this make God happy?"

PRAY TODAY

Dear God, please help me stop and think before I make decisions. I want to be good at following Your rules! Amen.

PRACTICE MAKES PATIENCE

Be gentle to everyone, able to teach, and patient.

2 TIMOTHY 2:24 HCSB

God talks about patience a lot in the Bible. It must be very important! But it's not always easy.

That's because patience takes lots of practice. Sometimes patience means waiting for someone to finish playing with a toy that you want. Sometimes it means not complaining while your mom or dad finishes shopping at the grocery store. Sometimes it means listening to someone else's story before you get to tell yours. Next time you feel impatient, take a deep breath and ask God to help you wait. That's practicing patience. And the more you practice, the better you'll be!

THOUGHT OF THE DAY

Think of a time you needed to be patient. What did you do?

PRAY TODAY

Dear God, I know You want me to be patient, but sometimes it's so hard. Please help me practice so I can get better! Amen.

GOD BEFORE STUFF

Seek first God's kingdom and what God wants. Then all your other needs will be met as well.

MATTHEW 6:33 NCV

It's normal to want stuff we don't have. Maybe a friend has a new toy you want to play with or a book you'd like to read. But trouble comes if you think about stuff more than you think about God!

Stuff is nice for a little while, but God is with you forever. He is more important than anything you could buy, and He has promised to take care of you! So don't worry about what you don't have. Spend time thanking God for what He has given you and doing things that make Him happy. You'll realize that stuff doesn't matter as much!

THOUGHT OF THE DAY

When you want something new, first thank God for what you already have!

PRAY TODAY

Dear God, thank You for everything You've given me! Help me focus on You instead of things. Amen.

HOW TO BE HAPPY

I will be happy because of you; God Most High, I will sing praises to your name.

PSALM 9:2 NCV

Did you know there's a secret to happiness? Thankfulness! It's true. Happiness comes from loving God and thanking Him for what He's done.

Try it! Think about all the good things God has given you. Do you love your family? Did you have fun with a friend today? Do you live in a comfy home? When you take time to thank God, it's hard to feel upset. That's because your mind is too full of God's goodness to let anything else in! So next time you feel grouchy, remember: happiness is just a few thank-yous away!

THOUGHT OF THE DAY

What are three things you're thankful for today?

PRAY TODAY

Dear God, thank You for everything You've done for me! I love thinking about You and praising You. Amen.

GIVE FREELY

Freely you have received; freely give.

MATTHEW 10:8 NIV

God has given you many gifts, but He doesn't expect anything back. Isn't that wonderful? That's what it means to "give freely." And He wants us to give freely to each other as well.

Think of what you can give to others. Of course, it's nice to give gifts on birthdays and Christmas, but you don't have to wait! Ask your parents how to give away nice toys or clothes you don't use anymore. Make a card to tell a friend how much you like them. And you can always give a hug to someone who feels sad. Giving gifts isn't about getting something back. It's about sharing God's love!

THOUGHT OF THE DAY

What is something you can give away today?

PRAY TODAY

Dear God, thank You for all the gifts You have given to me. Help me give to others like You have given to me! Amen.

IN LINE WITH JESUS

"Follow Me," Jesus told them, "and I will make you fish for people!" Immediately they left their nets and followed Him.

MARK 1:17–18 HCSB

When you're walking in a line, the first person leads everyone else where they should go. So, it's pretty important for that person to know the right way!

Jesus told people to follow Him because He knew the right way for them to go. He wanted His followers to care for others, showing people the way to God. He wanted them to make loving choices. As they followed Jesus, they were blessed, and they brought blessings to others too. It's a good idea to walk closely with Jesus every day. He knows the way to your very best life!

THOUGHT OF THE DAY

What's one thing you can do today that Jesus would do?

PRAY TODAY

Dear God, I want to follow Jesus every day of my life. Help me share His love with everyone I know. Amen.

GOD IS WITH YOU

"Do not fear, for I am with you; do not be afraid, for I am your God. I will strengthen you; I will help you; I will hold on to you with My righteous right hand."

ISAIAH 41:10 HCSB

Do you know that the Bible tells us exactly where God is? He's with you!

That might surprise you because you can't see God like you can see your mom or dad. But it's true! God promises that He will be with you no matter where you go, and God always keeps His promises. So you never need to feel lonely or afraid. God is bigger and stronger than anything, and He's by your side today, tomorrow, and forever.

THOUGHT OF THE DAY

With God beside you, you can do anything!

PRAY TODAY

Dear God, please help me remember that You are always with me. Thank You for keeping Your promises! Amen.

PATIENT AND FORGIVING

"Rebuke your brother if he sins, and forgive him if he is sorry. Even if he wrongs you seven times a day and each time turns again and asks forgiveness, forgive him."

LUKE 17:3-4 TLB

Do you ever feel like you make the same mistakes over and over? You're not alone! And just like God is loving and patient with you, sometimes you'll have to be patient with others.

One way you can show patience is by forgiving people when they apologize. Even if they've made the same mistake before, try not to get angry. Instead, think of apologies as cool opportunities to practice forgiveness! You can still be honest about how you feel, and thank them for saying sorry. Each time you forgive, you're helping someone learn that it's OK to try again.

THOUGHT OF THE DAY

Forgiveness is like a superpower—it makes everyone feel better!

PRAY TODAY

Dear God, please help me to be patient and forgiving, just like You are. Amen.

GOD'S TIMING

He has made everything beautiful in its time.

ECCLESIASTES 3:11 NIV

Sometimes God answers prayers quickly, and sometimes His answers take longer. Sometimes His answers look different from what you expect. But you can always be sure that God is working to give you the very best life.

It can be really hard to wait for something you want, but don't worry! You can spend that time looking for ways that God is already working. He is always doing great things! God has big, wonderful plans for you, and He knows exactly when everything should happen. So keep praying; then watch God's plans unfold.

THOUGHT OF THE DAY

God is always right on time!

PRAY TODAY

Dear God, sometimes I want things to happen right away. Please remind me that Your timing is perfect. Amen.

A JOYFUL HEART

A joyful heart is good medicine.

PROVERBS 17:22 HCSB

Can you remember the last time you laughed super hard? God wants you to have lots of moments like that! He is happiest when you have a joyful heart.

You can have a joyful heart by focusing on what makes you happy. Play a fun game with a sibling or tell your friend a funny joke. Turn on some music and have a dance party. You can even turn your chores into a game! If you look for it, you can find joy in every moment of your day. And that's exactly what God wants you to do!

THOUGHT OF THE DAY

What makes you laugh?

PRAY TODAY

Dear God, thank You for the gift of laughter. It always makes me feel better! Help me find joy all through my day. Amen.

HIS LOVE NEVER ENDS

The faithful love of the LORD never ends!

LAMENTATIONS 3:22 NLT

God's love is forever. You can always count on it. Nothing you do could ever make God love you less, and He will never lose His patience.

Lots of things eventually end. Clothes wear out, food goes bad in the fridge, and toys can get lost. But God's love isn't going anywhere. It's always here when you need it. And when you ask Jesus to live in your heart, He can help you feel and understand His love even more. That way, no matter where you go, you can remember that God's love is there too!

THOUGHT OF THE DAY

God loves you so much, no matter what, forever and ever.

PRAY TODAY

Dear God, wow! Your love is amazing! Thank You for loving me all the time, everywhere I go. Amen.

THE RIGHT TIME

There is a right time for everything. . . . A time to cry; a time to laugh; a time to grieve; a time to dance.

ECCLESIASTES 3:1, 4 TLB

No one feels the same way all the time. God knows that, and He tells us in the Bible that it's OK to have times when we feel sad and other times when we feel like laughing. Times when we get angry and other times when we feel like giving someone a hug. Feelings change, but one thing that never changes is God's love for us. It is always the right time for that!

THOUGHT OF THE DAY

God is good all the time! All the time God is good!

PRAY TODAY

Dear God, thank You for giving me so many feelings and for loving me all the time. Amen.

NEW THINGS

"For I am about to do something new. See, I have already begun! Do you not see it?"

ISAIAH 43:19 NLT

Sometimes it is fun to do new things like start a new grade in school, get a new pet, learn something new, or go to a new place. But doing new things can sometimes be scary too. Who will be there? Will you make a friend? How will you know what to do? God promises to be with us when we start new things. He loves to help us when we are not sure what to do or what will happen next. So when you have something new to do, remember that God is right there, helping you shine!

THOUGHT OF THE DAY

What's something new you're trying?

PRAY TODAY

Dear God, I'm glad that You are always with me, especially when I do new things. Amen.

THINK OF OTHERS FIRST

Don't be selfish. . . . Be humble, thinking of others as better than yourself.

PHILIPPIANS 2:3 TLB

Jesus was the most important person who ever lived. But He didn't brag, and He wasn't selfish. Instead, He thought of others' feelings before His own. That's called being humble.

God wants us to be humble too. You can be humble by letting someone else go before you in line or by being a good listener even when you want to say something. When you're humble, you show that God is most important. And it helps everyone around you feel good too!

THOUGHT OF THE DAY

To be humble, think about how others feel before you think about yourself.

PRAY TODAY

Dear God, it's not always easy to be humble. Please help me think of others first, just like Jesus did! Amen.

PRAISE GOD!

"The LORD is my strength and my song; He has become my salvation. This is my God, and I will praise Him."

EXODUS 15:2 HCSB

The Bible says it is important to praise God. But how do you do that?

You praise God when you thank Him for what He has done. You praise Him when you tell Him how much you love Him. You also praise God when you sing songs about how great He is. Praising God makes God happy. But it also makes us happy because praising God reminds us how amazing and wonderful He is. So whenever you want to feel extra joyful, just start praising God!

THOUGHT OF THE DAY

What are some ways you can praise God today?

PRAY TODAY

Dear God, You are great and mighty enough to make all the stars in the sky. Thank You for caring enough to love me! Amen.

EVERYTHING YOU NEED

And my God will supply every need of yours according to his riches in glory in Christ Jesus.

PHILIPPIANS 4:19 ESV

What's the difference between what you want and what you need? You might *want* a new bike or a special toy. But what do you really *need*? You need the love of your family, food to eat, a beautiful world to enjoy, sunlight, rain, and a safe place to live. Do you know who can give you all of those things? God can! The Bible reminds us that the earth and everything in it are His! God loves you, and He takes care of everything. You don't need to worry, because God has more than enough to give you all you need.

THOUGHT OF THE DAY

Can you name some of your needs that God has already provided?

PRAY TODAY

Dear God, thank You for taking care of all my needs. I will trust You and not worry. Amen.

GENTLE WORDS

Always be humble, gentle, and patient, accepting each other in love.

EPHESIANS 4:2 NCV

God asks us to speak gently to others. Gentle words are helpful, loving, and calm. It's not always easy to speak that way when you feel upset, but that's actually when gentleness is most needed! Kind, patient words can help everyone feel better.

There's nothing wrong with feeling upset or disagreeing with someone. Just remember to choose your words carefully. If you feel yourself getting angry, ask God to help you calm down. He can help you say things that will help and heal instead of hurt!

THOUGHT OF THE DAY

If you say something you wish you hadn't, you can still use gentle words to apologize!

PRAY TODAY

Dear God, sometimes it is SO hard to speak gently. Please help me to be calm and kind, even when I'm upset. Amen.

RESPECTFUL ACTIONS

Being respected is more important than having great riches.

PROVERBS 22:1 ICB

When you treat people with respect, you show them that they are valuable. In fact, the Bible says that respect is a better gift than riches!

Being polite is an excellent way to treat others with respect. Always share, say "please" and "thank you," and try not to interrupt when someone is talking. If your mom or dad or a teacher asks you to do something, do it right away instead of complaining. Say a kind word to someone, or just hold the door open for the person behind you. Even the smallest respectful action can make someone's day!

THOUGHT OF THE DAY

Choose a specific way to show respect to five people today.

PRAY TODAY

Dear God, I want to be respectful. Please help me treat everyone I meet with respect. Amen.

CHOOSE LIFE

I am offering you life or death, blessings or curses. Now, choose life! . . . To choose life is to love the LORD your God, obey him, and stay close to him.

DEUTERONOMY 30:19–20 NCV

God wants you to make good choices every day. But how can you know what choices are best?

Scripture gives us the answer: love God, obey Him, and stay close to Him. You can do these things by talking to God often, learning what He says in the Bible, and following His teachings. As we learn more about God and do what He says, it becomes easier and easier to make the best choices. That's how we choose life every single day!

THOUGHT OF THE DAY

What are some things you have to make choices about today?

PRAY TODAY

Dear God, every day I have choices to make. Help me choose to live the way You want me to. Amen.

CELEBRATE FRIENDS

Every time I think of you, I give thanks to my God.

PHILIPPIANS 1:3 NLT

Isn't it great to have friends? A good friend can cheer you up when you feel sad or share a laugh when you're feeling silly. Sometimes a friend can teach you how to do something new! And no matter how many friends you have, you can always make more.

Good friends are a gift from God, so remember to thank Him for all the special friends in your life. And be sure to tell your friends how much you love them too!

THOUGHT OF THE DAY

What are some things you like to do with your friends?

PRAY TODAY

Dear God, thank You for my friends. What a wonderful gift they are! Amen.

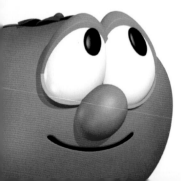

GIVE GOD JOY

And a voice from heaven said, "You are my dearly loved Son, and you bring me great joy."

MARK 1:11 NLT

D id you know that Jesus gave God joy? As Jesus grew, He showed God's love to others. He was kind, and He obeyed God. This made God very happy.

The Bible tells us that when we trust in Jesus as our Savior, we become children of God. He loves to see all His children helping others, being kind, and learning about Him. When you do your best to be like Jesus, you will also give God joy!

THOUGHT OF THE DAY

What do you think you can do today to bring God joy?

PRAY TODAY

Dear God, please help me to be more like Jesus. I want to bring You joy too. Amen.

A SPECIAL FRIEND

I will praise You because I have been remarkably and wonderfully made. Your works are wonderful, and I know this very well.

PSALM 139:14 HCSB

God made each person different, with unique talents, interests, and personalities. It would be so boring if we were all exactly alike!

You may know someone who has "special needs." Maybe they look or act different, or they can't do all the things most other kids can do. Remember that no matter what, everyone needs a good friend. After all, God loves everyone just as much as He loves you! So get to know someone who is different from you today. You might make a very special friend.

THOUGHT OF THE DAY

You may not understand why someone is different from you, so ask your parents privately. And always treat everyone like you'd want to be treated!

PRAY TODAY

Dear God, thank You for making us all so special. Help me show Your love to everyone! Amen.

SUPER POWER

Do not withhold good from those who deserve it when it's in your power to help them.

PROVERBS 3:27 NLT

Superheroes have many different powers. Some are very strong. Some can fly. Some can become invisible! But do you know that you have a special superpower too? The Bible says that you have the power to do something good for someone who needs help!

Whom do you know who could use some help today? Does your sister or brother need help learning something new? Does your mom or dad need you to help by doing your chores with a smile? Ask God to give you some ideas. Then use your superpower to help others today!

If you see a need, don't wait to be asked. Jump right in! That's how to be a superhero for God!

THOUGHT OF THE DAY

What can you do to help a friend or family member today?

PRAY TODAY

Dear God, thank You for giving me the superpower to be a great helper! Amen.

JUST AS YOU ARE

But God showed how much he loved us by having Christ die for us, even though we were sinful.

ROMANS 5:8 CEV

Jesus loves you just as you are. So don't worry about being perfect. No one is! You'll make mistakes and wrong choices, but Jesus' love will never change. He will never leave you, and He'll never stop listening to your prayers.

In fact, Jesus loves you so much that He gave His life so you could live with Him forever in heaven! All you have to do is say yes to His love. And when you say yes to Jesus, He'll show you how to share His love with others too. Since nobody's perfect, everyone needs Jesus' love.

THOUGHT OF THE DAY

Jesus lived a perfect life so we don't have to!

PRAY TODAY

Dear Jesus, thank You for loving me enough to give Your life for me. I know I'm not perfect—and I'm glad I don't need to be! Amen.

CHOOSE KINDNESS

Love is patient, love is kind.

1 CORINTHIANS 13:4 HCSB

We know that kindness is always best. But if you're feeling sad or angry, you might not feel like caring for anyone else! Still, God tells us to love one another all the time. And that means acting kind even when you don't feel like it.

But here's a secret. When you do a kind act, you'll start to feel a little love! The more kind things you do, the more love you will feel. Try it out! You'll be surprised how your feelings can change when you choose kindness.

THOUGHT OF THE DAY

A kind act can be small. Who is someone you can show kindness to today?

PRAY TODAY

Dear God, help me choose kindness all the time. I want to love like You love! Amen.

A PURE HEART

Create in me a pure heart, God, and make my spirit right again.

PSALM 51:10 NCV

When you look at someone else, what do you see? Do they have curly hair? Are they tall or short? You can see only what's on the outside, but God sees what is on the inside of each person. He sees your feelings. He knows what makes you happy or angry or afraid.

The Bible calls what is inside each person their "heart" or "spirit." When you are feeling sad or mad, your spirit doesn't feel right. The Bible says that when this happens, you can ask God to make your heart clean and your spirit right again. God cares about you, so He wants you to have a happy heart!

THOUGHT OF THE DAY

How is your heart feeling today?

PRAY TODAY

Dear God, thank You for knowing me on the inside. Please give me a pure and happy heart. Amen.

TRUE FRIENDS

A friend loves you all the time.

PROVERBS 17:17 ICB

Bob and Larry have been friends for a long time! Longtime friends go through hard times, and they sometimes get annoyed, but they still stay friends. That's who God wants you to be: a true friend!

The Bible says that a true friend loves all the time. That means you keep on loving even when you're irritated or tired or when things seem really hard. True friends lift each other up in difficult times, just like God lifts you up. So thank God for the friends in your life! And look for ways to lift them up today.

THOUGHT OF THE DAY

True friendship is a wonderful gift!

PRAY TODAY

Dear God, thank You for being the best friend of all! Help me to be a true friend today and every day. Amen.

YOU'RE SO VERY SPECIAL

"I have loved you with a love that lasts forever. I have kept on loving you with a kindness that never fails."

JEREMIAH 31:3B NIRV

No one else in the entire world is exactly like you. God made you to have a unique set of talents, ideas, feelings, and thoughts. The world needs you to be you!

You might have days when you wish you could be like someone else. Of course, you can learn from people you admire, like teachers, leaders, and your parents. But remember that you are important to God because of who YOU are. If you ever feel like you're not special, just talk to God. He can't wait to show you how amazing and wonderful you truly are.

THOUGHT OF THE DAY

Can you think of three things that make you special and unique?

PRAY TODAY

Dear God, thank You for making me the way I am. Help me remember that I am very important to You! Amen.

HOW TO BE A FRIEND

Love each other with genuine affection, and take delight in honoring each other.

ROMANS 12:10 NLT

One of God's best gifts is the gift of friendship. Who are some of your friends?

The Bible reminds us to love our friends and show them honor. This means thinking about what they would like to do, sharing with them, and helping them. Good friends take turns and find ways to make each other happy. Friends cheer each other up when they are sad and celebrate with one another when they are happy. Friends who honor one another build friendships that last a long time. If you want to *have* a good friend, learn to *be* a good friend!

THOUGHT OF THE DAY

What are some good ways to honor your friends today?

PRAY TODAY

Dear God, thank You for my friends! Help me to be the kind of friend I want to have. Amen.

GOD KEEPS HIS PROMISES

Those who know Your name will put their trust in You. For You, O Lord, have never left alone those who look for You.

PSALM 9:10 NLV

Sometimes it's easy to see God working in your life. But other times, it's hard to know what He's up to. Maybe you didn't get on a team you'd hoped to join, or a good friend moved away and you feel lonely. Maybe you prayed for something, and it didn't happen. Don't worry—God still hears you! Remember God's good promises: He loves you, He listens to you, He'll never leave you, and He has good plans for you. God never breaks a promise. So keep on praying, and keep on trusting. He is always by your side.

THOUGHT OF THE DAY

Jesus loves you, this you know. He will never let you go.

PRAY TODAY

Dear God, I trust that You're with me. When I'm having a hard day, please remind me of all Your good promises. Amen.

COURAGE TO WAIT

Wait patiently for the LORD. Be brave and courageous. Yes, wait patiently for the LORD.

PSALM 27:14 NLT

We usually think of courage as doing something scary like facing a lion or defeating a giant. But the Bible says it also takes courage to wait! When you are trying to learn to ride a bike or read or jump rope, it takes courage to be patient, keep trying, and not give up. When you're not old enough to do something you want to do, it takes courage to wait until you're ready. You have to believe that God will help you learn, grow, and do great things! It's not always easy to wait, but ask God for help. He wants you to be courageous!

THOUGHT OF THE DAY
Where do you need to have courage to wait today?

PRAY TODAY
Dear God, please help me to have the courage to wait patiently to learn the things You want me to know. Amen.

LOVE YOU

God began doing a good work in you, and I am sure he will continue it until it is finished when Jesus Christ comes again.

PHILIPPIANS 1:6 NCV

We know God wants us to be loving and kind to everyone. But there's someone you might forget: you! God wants you to love yourself too!

You are very special to God, so He wants to make sure you treat yourself with love and respect. If you make a mistake, forgive yourself. If you're having a hard time with something, be patient with yourself. God is hard at work doing good things in and around you. You can help Him by appreciating all He made you to be!

THOUGHT OF THE DAY

If you want to love others as you love yourself, you have to love yourself!

PRAY TODAY

Dear God, help me see myself like You see me. Thank You for showing me what love looks like. Amen.

GOOD MEDICINE

A cheerful heart is good medicine, but a broken spirit saps a person's strength.

PROVERBS 17:22 NLT

If you get an earache or you have a bad cough, the doctor might give you medicine to help you get better. Did you know that there is a special kind of medicine that you can give your friends who are feeling sad or lonely? The Bible says, "A cheerful heart is good medicine"! That's because sharing a smile, a laugh, or even a hug reminds others that you care about them. And that makes anyone feel great! A gift of cheer is good medicine. And you don't even have to go to the doctor!

THOUGHT OF THE DAY

Can you think of someone who needs some cheering up? What can you do for them today?

PRAY TODAY

Dear God, please help me find ways to help someone feel better today. Amen.

JOY THAT NEVER ENDS

A cheerful heart has a continual feast.

PROVERBS 15:15 HCSB

Imagine being at a great party that never ends! The Bible says having a cheerful heart is just like that—plenty of good things and joy to last forever.

Look around and see all the wonderful gifts God has given you: family, friends, sunshine, stars, singing birds, and good food to eat. When you choose to have a cheerful heart and to think about all the loving gifts God has given to you, your joy will never end. So even when things don't go the way you want, always choose to celebrate the good things you have!

THOUGHT OF THE DAY

What are some of the wonderful gifts God has given you?

PRAY TODAY

Dear God, help me remember to rejoice in Your amazing love all the time. Amen.

WHAT'S YOUR STORY?

All who worship God, come here and listen; I will tell you everything God has done for me.

PSALM 66:16 CEV

If you know God, then you have a story to tell! Has God ever answered one of your prayers? Has He helped you to be brave when you were afraid? Has He helped you get better when you were sick? When someone wonders about who God is and what He does, tell your story. You can talk about how God loves everyone. You can share how He listens to prayers and answers them. You can tell a story about one of the ways He helped you. When you tell your story, you help others to know and trust God.

THOUGHT OF THE DAY
What story will you tell about God?

PRAY TODAY
Dear God, thank You for all the many things You have done for me. Please help me share my story with my friends. Amen.

DO IT GOD'S WAY!

But Jesus said, "Those who hear the teaching of God and obey it—they are the ones who are truly blessed."

LUKE 11:28 ICB

The Bible tells the amazing story of a man named Joshua. God told Joshua to lead His people into the city of Jericho. But there was a huge wall around the city to keep out armies like Joshua's. God didn't say to climb over it or tear it down. Instead, He said the army should march around the city seven times and then blow their trumpets and shout. That's it! It sounded strange, but Joshua convinced everyone to obey God. When they did exactly what God said, the walls crumbled and fell! That day, everyone saw that obeying God is always the best idea.

THOUGHT OF THE DAY

Obey God, even if His directions seem strange. Then watch what amazing things He does!

PRAY TODAY

Dear God, help me trust Your directions, even when I think I have a better idea. Amen.

THINK FIRST!

Enthusiasm without knowledge is not good. If you act too quickly, you might make a mistake.

PROVERBS 19:2 NCV

It's fun to be playful and get excited about new ideas. But sometimes we do things without thinking, and not-so-good things can happen. God encourages us to slow down sometimes and think things through.

When you think of something you want to do or a feeling you want to express, think about what could happen next. If you run outside without shoes on, what might you step on? If you shout at someone, how will they feel? When you take just a moment to think first, you can make wiser choices. You'll be safer, and everyone will have more fun!

THOUGHT OF THE DAY

Can you think of a time you acted without thinking first? What happened?

PRAY TODAY

Dear God, please help me slow down so I can make wise choices. I don't need to be in a hurry all the time! Amen.

HOW TO FIND GOD

"But from there you will search for the LORD your God, and you will find Him when you seek Him with all your heart and all your soul."

DEUTERONOMY 4:29 HCSB

Have you ever played hide-and-seek with a friend? You close your eyes and count while your friend hides, and then you say, "Ready or not, here I come!" Then you look everywhere you can think of to find your friend. God makes it easy for us to find Him anytime we want! All we have to do is *want* to find Him. We can read about Him in our Bibles. We can hear about Him at church. We can talk to Him any time we want. God never hides from us. He always wants us to find Him.

THOUGHT OF THE DAY

How do you look for God?

PRAY TODAY

Dear God, thank You for always being near and for making it easy for me to find You anytime I want. Amen.

SURPRISING PAYBACK

Don't repay evil for evil. Don't snap back at those who say unkind things about you. Instead, pray for God's help for them, for we are to be kind to others, and God will bless us for it.

1 PETER 3:9 TLB

When someone does something nice for you, it makes you feel good. You may want to do something nice for them too! But what should you do when someone does or says something unkind?

God's response might surprise you. He wants you to do good to everyone, all the time! If someone says a mean thing, the best thing you can do is say something kind in return. Maybe they just need someone to show them how to be kind! It's not what everyone expects you to do. It's God's way, and God's way is always best!

THOUGHT OF THE DAY
Kindness is the best surprise of all!

PRAY TODAY
Dear God, help me surprise someone with kindness today! Amen.

BE A HAPPY HELPER

Do everything without complaining and arguing.

PHILIPPIANS 2:14 NLT

God wants us to be happy helpers. That means we should follow directions right away and without arguing.

When a parent or teacher asks you to do something, you have a choice. You can say, "Sure! I can do that!" Or you can say, "Aw, do I have to?" Which do you think would make God glad?

Following directions the first time we are asked makes everyone happier. It also shows that we are doing what God wants us to do—helping without complaining. So next time your mom or dad asks you to do something, put on a smile and be a happy helper!

THOUGHT OF THE DAY

Smile first, then respond. That's the first step to being a happy helper!

PRAY TODAY

Dear God, sometimes it's hard to follow directions. Please help me stay away from arguing so I can be happy instead. Amen!

PERFECT PEACE

You keep him in perfect peace whose mind is stayed on you, because he trusts in you.

ISAIAH 26:3 ESV

The Bible says that if we spend our time thinking about how wonderful God is, then God will give us His perfect peace. Why is His peace perfect? Because God knows everything, and He loves you very much. So when you trust in God, you can be sure He is taking care of you, no matter what.

The best way to hold on to God's peace is to think about Him all the time. Pray every day, and read your Bible too. Fill your mind with God. Then God will fill you up with peace!

THOUGHT OF THE DAY

Trade your worries for God's perfect peace.

PRAY TODAY

Dear God, thank You for Your perfect peace. I will trust You and think about all You have done for me. Amen.

GOD'S GOT THIS

Since God assured us, "I'll never let you down, never walk off and leave you," we can boldly quote, "God is there, ready to help; I'm fearless no matter what. Who or what can get to me?"

HEBREWS 13:5–6 MSG

Is something bothering you? Maybe there's a problem you can't solve or a bad habit you can't seem to break? Give it to God! Nothing is too hard for Him.

God knows how to handle every problem. But His solutions aren't always what we expect—they're usually much better than anything we could imagine! Even if you think you've tried everything, ask God to help you try again. Even if you think there's no solution, give God a chance. Trust His power, and see what He does. He's got this!

THOUGHT OF THE DAY

Ask God to help you solve what's bothering you. Then watch what happens!

PRAY TODAY

Dear God, thank You for taking care of me! I'm so glad nothing is too hard for You. Amen.

PLAY FAIR AND WIN!

Happiness comes to those who are fair to others and are always just and good.

PSALM 106:3 TLB

Everyone enjoys winning games. It can even be tempting to do something that will help you win unfairly. But that's not really winning.

God wants us to play fair because it's right and kind. Cheating robs others of a good game! Instead, practice having a positive attitude whether you win or lose. If you win, thank everyone for playing with you and tell them you had fun. If you lose, you can congratulate the winner and ask to play again sometime. Everyone likes to play with someone who plays fair and keeps things fun!

THOUGHT OF THE DAY

Win or lose, you can still have a lot of fun!

PRAY TODAY

Dear God, help me resist the temptation to cheat. Give me a good attitude, whether or not I win. Amen.

A HAPPY LIFE

Be satisfied with what you have. For God has said, "I will never fail you. I will never abandon you."

HEBREWS 13:5 NLT

Some people think they can have a happy life only if they always get their way or if they get all the things they want. But that's not how happiness works. True happiness comes from God!

When we spend time wishing we had different things, we make ourselves unhappy. Instead, trust God to give you what you need, and enjoy the blessings He's already given you. When you trust Him, He can fill you with His joy and peace. There won't be room for anything else but happiness!

THOUGHT OF THE DAY

Look around you. What can you be happy about right now?

PRAY TODAY

Dear God, thank You for caring for me. Please help me find happiness in You. Amen.

A JOYFUL GIVER

God loves the person who gives happily.

2 CORINTHIANS 9:7 ICB

God is so happy when you share your time and things with others. It's a great way to praise Him and get to know Him better. But don't just give—give happily!

Giving to others should make us glad because we're doing what God wants. We're also meeting new people and learning about them, which is fun! Be careful not to give with the goal of getting something back. Instead, give with a kind and open heart, excited to see what God does. When you give happily, God can do amazing things through you!

THOUGHT OF THE DAY

There are lots of ways to give to others. Find one that makes you happy!

PRAY TODAY

Dear God, thank You for my blessings. Help me share them joyfully! Amen.

TIME WELL SPENT

But when you pray, go into your private room, shut your door, and pray to your Father who is in secret.

MATTHEW 6:6 HCSB

How do you grow closer to your friends? You spend time with them! You probably play together and talk about things that matter to you. If you want to get to know someone, you have to spend time together.

Don't forget that God is your friend too. He wants to spend time with you so that you can know Him better and learn to trust Him more.

Set aside time every day to talk to your very best friend. Before long, you'll start to feel as close to God as you feel to the rest of your friends!

THOUGHT OF THE DAY

Find a comfy space to use especially for talking to God. It can be your special Prayer Place!

PRAY TODAY

Dear God, help me set aside time every day to spend with You. I want for us to become better friends! Amen.

NOTHING LEFT TO FEAR

There is no fear in love, but perfect love casts out fear.

1 JOHN 4:18 ESV

God knows that sometimes we all feel afraid. But He also wants us to know that He can help. The Bible says that God's perfect love makes fear go away. But how?

When we fill up our minds with thoughts about how much God loves us, there isn't enough room for thoughts about being afraid. Fear has to leave when God's love shows up! Why not give it a try? The next time you feel afraid, think about God's amazing love—how big it is and how powerful it is. Thank God for loving you, and see if your fearful thoughts start to disappear.

THOUGHT OF THE DAY

Name some ways God shows His wonderful love to you.

PRAY TODAY

Dear God, thank You for Your perfect love that is bigger than my fears. Amen.

A PEACEFUL FAMILY

How wonderful, how beautiful, when brothers and sisters get along!

PSALM 133:1 MSG

Do you ever feel frustrated at home? It happens to all of us! Maybe you have a brother or sister who gets into your things sometimes. Even though you love them very much, it's not unusual to argue now and then.

A home full of anger is no fun. So if you find yourself arguing, ask God to help you bring peace to the situation instead. That might mean suggesting something different that everyone can agree on, or sometimes being willing to give up what you want to do. Seeking peace is a good thing, and sometimes you have to work at it.

THOUGHT OF THE DAY

A peaceful home means more room for fun!

PRAY TODAY

Dear God, please help me seek Your peace, even when I feel frustrated. Amen.

GOD'S PROTECTION

The LORD himself watches over you! The LORD stands beside you as your protective shade.

PSALM 121:5 NLT

God promises He will always watch over you. He never takes a break or stops paying attention, day or night. That means you can always count on God's help and protection!

Things may not always go the way you want, but no matter what happens, you're never alone. Sometimes God protects you by saying no to something you ask for, because He has a better plan. He may protect you from things you don't even know about! So trust that God is in control. You are never out of His sight.

THOUGHT OF THE DAY

God protects your heart from fear. Trust that He is always here!

PRAY TODAY

Dear God, thank You that You're always looking out for me. Please protect me today! Amen.

YOUR BEST FRIEND

"You are my friends if you obey me. Servants don't know what their master is doing, and so I don't speak to you as servants. I speak to you as my friends, and I have told you everything that my Father has told me."

JOHN 15:14–15 CEV

Do you have a best friend? Best friends help each other. They always stick up for one another. They care about one another and spend time together having fun. Guess what? Jesus wants to be your best friend! He will always help you and care for you. He always tells you the truth, and He never leaves you all alone. When we do what Jesus says to do, like loving God, praying, and helping others, we show that Jesus is our best friend too. Isn't it great to have a best friend like Jesus?

THOUGHT OF THE DAY

Be sure to talk with Jesus every day! Talking together is how friends become *best* friends.

PRAY TODAY

Dear God, thank You for being my very best friend. I love You, and I want to be a good friend to You too! Amen.

TWO LITTLE WORDS

Admit your faults . . . and pray for each other so that you may be healed.

JAMES 5:16 TLB

Why is it so hard to apologize sometimes? Maybe you feel proud and don't want to admit that you were wrong. Maybe you feel embarrassed. Maybe you're worried you'll get in trouble. But be brave! Two of the most powerful words you can ever say are "I'm sorry." Those words can heal hurt feelings. And they can build really strong friendships! So don't be afraid of saying you're sorry. Do it right away, and watch what God does with those two little words!

THOUGHT OF THE DAY

Even if what happened was an accident, it's important to say you're sorry. Then the healing can begin!

PRAY TODAY

Dear God, thank You that You always forgive me. Help me say "I'm sorry" to others and ask for their forgiveness too. Amen.

ONE THING AT A TIME

Tell me in the morning about your love, because I trust you. Show me what I should do, because my prayers go up to you.

PSALM 143:8 NCV

Some days there is so much to do, we don't know where to start. But Jesus can help!

Start the day right by asking Jesus to show you what needs to be done first. He can help you see what's most important. When you let Jesus lead you, He will help you care about the things He cares about. That way, you and Jesus can work together all day long. What a great day that will be!

THOUGHT OF THE DAY

Make a list of what you need to do; then pray about what to do first. It's fun to cross things off as you finish them.

PRAY TODAY

Dear God, please show me what to do each day. Thank You for always helping me. Amen.

KEEP BURNING!

Don't burn out; keep yourselves fueled and aflame. Be alert servants of the Master, cheerfully expectant. Don't quit in hard times; pray all the harder.

ROMANS 12:11-12 MSG

School, sports, lessons, and time with friends are fun and important. But sometimes we can get so busy that we don't spend time with God or talk to God.

Talking with God will help you to follow His ways. Thanking Him for your blessings will also help you enjoy your life. You might even feel like you have more energy! God will help you keep your energy going so you can keep shining His love in the world and in your heart as you talk to Him each day.

THOUGHT OF THE DAY

Make sure to make time for your relationship with God. Remember that God is most important!

PRAY TODAY

Dear God, help me to spend time with You every day. Nothing is more important than our friendship! Amen.

HAVING FUN

"He will yet fill your mouth with laughter and your lips with shouts of joy."

JOB 8:21 NIV

What makes you laugh? A tickle on your toes? A funny joke? A silly picture? God loves to see His children laugh. It makes Him happy to know that you are happy! Today, see if you can find something to laugh about. Maybe you will see a friend making a silly face or hear a funny story or sing a song with silly words. Maybe you'll make others laugh too! Laughing and having fun are both ways to show that we're filled with joy. When we are happy, that makes God happy too!

THOUGHT OF THE DAY

What kinds of things make you laugh?

PRAY TODAY

Dear God, thank You for loving me and for wanting me to be filled with joy! Amen.

GIFTS FROM GOD

Whatever is good and perfect is a gift coming down to us from God our Father, who created all the lights in the heavens.

JAMES 1:17A NLT

You are God's child! And do you know that God gives all His children good gifts? They're not tied up in shiny paper and ribbons. You don't even need to unwrap them. You just need to look around. Some of God's gifts are small, like a tiny flower or a beautiful butterfly. Some of God's gifts are huge like a snowy mountain or a colorful rainbow. Some of God's gifts are invisible like your mother's love or your daddy's laugh. God loves to give all His children wonderful gifts every single day, so look around and see what He has given to you!

THOUGHT OF THE DAY

What are some of your favorite God-gifts?

PRAY TODAY

Dear God, thank You for loving me and giving me wonderful gifts every day. Amen.

SERVING OTHERS

"I tell you the truth, anything you did for even the least of my people here, you also did for me."

MATTHEW 25:40 NCV

Does it sometimes feel like Jesus is far away? The Bible tells us that when we help someone in need, it's like we're helping Jesus Himself! So a great way to feel closer to God is to find a way to help others.

It can be something for one person, like making a card for a sick friend or helping your mom clean up. Or you can ask your parents or your church how to do something for a big group of people. Whatever you do, do it with a glad heart because you are serving Jesus!

THOUGHT OF THE DAY

When you help people, you show them that Jesus loves them.

PRAY TODAY

Dear God, please show me how I can help others. I want to make You glad! Amen.

FOLLOW HIS VOICE

"My sheep hear My voice, and I know them, and they follow Me."

JOHN 10:27 NKJV

Shepherds protect and guide flocks of sheep. A good shepherd never leaves his or her sheep alone. The sheep learn to recognize their shepherd's voice, telling them where to go.

Jesus tells us that He is our Good Shepherd. So we should follow His voice! But what does Jesus' voice sound like? Maybe it's an idea to make friends with a new kid. Maybe it's a calm feeling when you'd normally be afraid. Maybe it's a reminder to forgive even though you feel angry. When you read your Bible and pray, you'll get to know Jesus' voice more and more. Then you'll always know which way to go!

THOUGHT OF THE DAY

Just like a shepherd, Jesus will never leave you. So listen for His voice everywhere!

PRAY TODAY

Dear Jesus, thank You for being my Good Shepherd. Help me learn to hear Your voice! Amen.

SING TO THE LORD!

Shout with joy to the LORD, all the earth! Worship the LORD with gladness. Come before him, singing with joy.

PSALM 100:1–2 NLT

Do you like to sing? Have you ever felt so happy that you just had to sing a song? Singing, playing musical instruments, clapping your hands, and dancing are all wonderful ways to show your joy!

When we see the beautiful world God has created and all the ways God has blessed us with family and friends, sometimes our joy just bubbles out! So when you're happy and you know it, shout for joy! God loves to hear how glad you are to be His child.

THOUGHT OF THE DAY

What is your favorite song about Jesus?

PRAY TODAY

Dear God, thank You for making me Your child and giving me so many good things. Help me celebrate You today! Amen.

TIME FOR GOD

Be gracious to me, Lord, for I call to You all day long.

PSALM 86:3 HCSB

Do you know that you can talk to God any time of the day or night? Some people like to pray and read their Bibles in the morning. Others read Bible stories before bed. Some folks gather with friends or family to have a time called "devotions," when they read Bible verses together and talk about what they mean.

Because God is always there, you can talk, pray, or read about Him any time you want. Making time for God every day is the best way to help your faith grow and for you to become better friends with Him!

THOUGHT OF THE DAY

When do you like to spend time praying and talking with God?

PRAY TODAY

Dear God, I'm so glad I can talk to You every day. Thank You for always being there for me. Amen.

LOVE YOUR ENEMY

"There is a saying, 'Love your friends and hate your enemies.' But I say: Love your enemies! Pray for those who persecute you!"

MATTHEW 5:43-44 TLB

Jesus says some pretty surprising things. But maybe the most surprising is "love your enemies!" Why should we love people we don't even like very much? Especially if they aren't nice to us!

Jesus knows that selfless love can change anything. It can help lonely people feel cared for. It can calm someone's anger. It can introduce someone to God. It can even turn enemies into friends. When you have the chance to show love to someone, always do it. It can be as easy as a kind word or a shared snack. You never know what will happen!

THOUGHT OF THE DAY

Is there someone you know who is hard to love? How can you love them today?

PRAY TODAY

Dear God, You love everyone. Help me love everyone too. Amen.

SHARE WHAT YOU HAVE

Do not neglect to do good and to share what you have, for such sacrifices are pleasing to God.

HEBREWS 13:16 ESV

Nobody has everything. But everybody has something! And when we share the things we have, everyone can enjoy a little more.

God asks us to share the things we have. Think about all the things you can share with others! When you play with a friend, you can share your toys so you'll both have more fun. If someone at school doesn't have a snack, you can ask if they want to share yours. Sharing makes people feel loved and cared for. And that makes God happy too!

THOUGHT OF THE DAY

Think of a time someone shared something with you. How did that make you feel?

PRAY TODAY

Dear God, please show me the things I can share with others. Then help me share them joyfully! Amen.

HIS PROMISES ARE GUARANTEED

"Do not be afraid or discouraged. For the LORD your God is with you wherever you go."

JOSHUA 1:9 NLT

The stories in the Bible tell us something wonderful: God keeps His promises! What are God's promises? God loves you. He gives strength to people when they feel weak or afraid. He always hears your prayers. He will give you everything you need. Nothing will ever separate you from God's love. And because of Jesus, we can live with Him forever in heaven. Those are some pretty big promises!

Sometimes people make big promises they can't keep. That can be disappointing! But you never have to worry about that with God. His promises are guaranteed!

THOUGHT OF THE DAY
God's promises are always true; He's watching out for me and you!

PRAY TODAY
Dear God, thank You for always keeping Your promises! I know that I can trust You. Amen.

WHAT TIME IS IT?

There is a time for everything. . . . a time to be silent and a time to speak.

ECCLESIASTES 3:1, 7 NIV

The Bible says sometimes it is important to be silent and listen, and other times it is important to talk. Some listening times are when you are at school or at church and another person is telling you a story. Some talking times are when it is your turn to share about something you know or when you have something important to tell a friend or your mom and dad. We learn about things by talking *and* by listening. It's important to know what time it is!

THOUGHT OF THE DAY

If you want others to listen to you, you should also be a good listener!

PRAY TODAY

Dear God, thank You for always listening to me. Help me know when I should talk and when I should listen. Amen.

VISITING GOD'S HOUSE

"For where two or three are gathered together in My name, I am there among them."

Matthew 18:20 HCSB

Isn't it fun to visit a friend's house? You get to know them better and play together too.

The Bible says that church is God's house. That makes sense! It is where you go to spend time with God and other people who are also God's children. When you go to church, you hear stories about God, sing songs about His love, and learn about the best way to live. The next time you go to church, think about all the wonderful things you can do at God's house. Then thank Him for inviting you to visit!

THOUGHT OF THE DAY

What is your favorite thing to do at church?

PRAY TODAY

Dear God, thanks for inviting me to Your house. Help me pay attention and learn everything I can about You. Amen.

THINKING LIKE JESUS

Make your own attitude that of Christ Jesus.

PHILIPPIANS 2:5 HCSB

The way you think is called your "attitude." The Bible says we should try to have the same attitude as Jesus. We can know how Jesus thought by listening to stories about Him and reading what He said in the Bible. Jesus loved others and said they were important. Jesus didn't worry about things because He trusted God to give Him all He needed. Jesus looked for what was good, even when things didn't go the way He wanted. And guess what? You can choose to think the same way Jesus did!

THOUGHT OF THE DAY

Things look brighter every day when you think the "Jesus way"!

PRAY TODAY

Dear God, please help me have a Jesus attitude. I want to learn to think more like Him. Amen.

YOU CAN DO IT!

As Goliath moved closer to attack, David quickly ran out to meet him.

1 SAMUEL 17:48 NLT

Did you know that God wants to do His work in you and through you? And God's work is always great! Even though you're just one person, He wants your life to be a full life of serving Him and His plan in the world.

The Bible is full of surprising people who changed the world. David was the smallest son in a big family, but he saved a whole army! Esther was a poor orphan who became a powerful queen. Mary came from a small town, but God chose her to be Jesus' mother. God can use anyone to do His work, and that includes you. God can use you to do great things!

THOUGHT OF THE DAY

Do your best, trust God, and watch what He does!

PRAY TODAY

Dear God, thank You that You will do great things with me! Amen.

LIVE IN PEACE

It is good and pleasant when God's people live together in peace!

PSALM 133:1 NCV

Every day you get to decide how you'll act with the people you meet. So why not decide to get along? When you get along with others, that's called living peacefully.

If a friend wants to play something different, give it a try! When you meet someone new, say hello with a smile. If someone says something mean, choose to respond with kind words instead of angry ones. You might meet people who like to argue instead of being peaceful. Don't worry! You still get to control how YOU act. And who knows? You might just convince them to give peace a chance too!

THOUGHT OF THE DAY

What's one way you can brighten someone's day today?

PRAY TODAY

Dear God, please help me get along with the people around me. I want to live peacefully with everyone! Amen.

FINDING YOUR TALENTS

God has given each of you a gift from his great variety of spiritual gifts. Use them well to serve one another.

1 PETER 4:10 NLT

What do you love to do? Do you enjoy telling stories or playing sports or playing music? Or maybe you can't wait to play with animals or learn about science!

No matter what you do, give thanks to God. God gives each of us special gifts and abilities, which are sometimes called "talents." Think about what your talents might be and then work hard to get better at them! When you do, God can use you in amazing ways to serve others and share His love. And that's the greatest gift of all!

THOUGHT OF THE DAY

How can you use your talents to serve others?

PRAY TODAY

Dear God, thank You for the talents You've given me. Help me work hard so You can do great things through me! Amen.

GOD'S GIFT OF PEACE

Only God gives inward peace, and I depend on him.

PSALM 62:5 CEV

The Bible says a lot about peace. That's because it's a wonderful gift that only God can give!

The peace that God promises is something He gives you. He is in control of everything, and He wants you to live every day knowing that, both in your head and your heart. Anytime you feel afraid, you can hand Him all your worries and trust Him to take care of you. And since God's peace lives inside you, you will never lose it. What a great gift!

THOUGHT OF THE DAY

God can help you anytime and anywhere. He wants to give you peace inside your heart and mind.

PRAY TODAY

Dear God, thank You for the gift of peace.
Help me feel it today! Amen.

DON'T WORRY, BE HAPPY!

Worry is a heavy burden, but a kind word always brings cheer.

PROVERBS 12:25 CEV

What's it like when you feel worried about something? Do you have trouble sleeping or feel grouchy all day? The Bible tells us that worrying is like carrying a heavy bag around all the time. It's no fun!

But guess what? You can give that heavy bag to God! Nothing is too heavy for Him, and you'll be surprised by how much lighter you feel. When you hand your worries to God, you'll be able to focus on more important things like having fun with friends and sharing His love!

THOUGHT OF THE DAY

Ask God to take your worries away; then focus your thinking on helping someone else!

PRAY TODAY

Dear God, thank You that nothing is too heavy for You to carry. Please help me give my worries to You. Amen.

A POWERFUL LIFE

For the kingdom of God is not a matter of talk but of power.

1 CORINTHIANS 4:20 NIV

God wants you to live an "empowered life." That means you don't just sit around and talk about things you wish would happen. It means you *make* things happen!

Choosing to follow God is the first step to an empowered life. God can give you courage to try new things and make new friends. He can give you joy, even when bad things happen. He can show you how to help people around you in new, creative ways. So what do you want to do? Ask God for the power to do it!

THOUGHT OF THE DAY

God's power has no limits—so neither should your ideas!

PRAY TODAY

Dear God, thank You for sharing Your power with me! Help me make exciting things happen in Your name! Amen.

THE WORRY BOX

Give all your worries and cares to God, for he cares about you.

1 PETER 5:7 NLT

God wants you to give Him anything you're worried about. He is bigger and stronger than anything, and He can help you if you let Him.

But what does it look like to give God your worries? Try this: Find a shoebox and ask a grown-up to help you cut a hole in the top. Any time you feel worried about something, write or draw it on a piece of paper. Then say a prayer telling God your worries, and drop the paper in the box. Once your worry is out of sight, imagine God taking it away. Now it's in His hands!

THOUGHT OF THE DAY

Give God your worries and your fear. He can make them disappear!

PRAY TODAY

Dear God, I know You don't want me to spend time worrying. Help me remember to give everything to You! Amen.

TALK IT OUT

Those who are sad now are happy. God will comfort them.

MATTHEW 5:4 ICB

Everybody feels sad sometimes. The best thing you can do when you feel sad is talk to God. God understands your heart and your mind, and He wants to comfort you. If you share your feelings with God, He can start to help you feel better.

Another good thing to do is talk to your parents. They may have felt just like you do and can share some wisdom and advice. Or sometimes you just need someone to listen while you talk through stuff. Your mom or dad can be that person too. Putting your feelings into words is the first step to feeling better!

THOUGHT OF THE DAY

If it's hard to talk about your feelings, try writing them down or drawing a picture.

PRAY TODAY

Dear God, please help me remember I can talk to my parents and to You whenever I feel sad. Amen.

BUILD SELF-CONTROL

To your knowledge, add self-control; and to your self-control, add patience.

2 PETER 1:6 NCV

When you want something, you probably want it right away. But that's not usually how things work! That's where patience and self-control come in. God wants us to learn self-control because He knows good things take time. And hurrying causes mistakes! If you don't practice, you won't learn to play an instrument or perform a dance well. If you push someone out of line so you can go first, you'll probably get in trouble. So ask God to help you build self-control. He will give you strength and patience so you can grow and learn all you need to!

THOUGHT OF THE DAY

Next time you want to rush through something, stop and ask God to help you go slow!

PRAY TODAY

Dear God, please help me build self-control so I can learn new things and be a good friend! Amen.

HOW TO BE STRONG

Finally, be strong in the Lord and in his mighty power.

EPHESIANS 6:10 NIV

People do all kinds of things to be strong. They exercise to build their muscles. They eat healthy food and get plenty of sleep. All of this helps make their bodies strong, but did you know there is another kind of strength? Being strong in the Lord is even more important than having strong muscles.

We get strong in the Lord by reading our Bibles, praying, and doing what God says. If you ask Him, God will teach you to follow Him and trust Him, and you will grow stronger each day. Nothing is greater than God's power. With Him, nothing is impossible!

THOUGHT OF THE DAY

Build your faith muscles by reading your Bible every day!

PRAY TODAY

Dear God, please help me learn to trust You more so I can be strong in You. Amen.

BRING OUT THE BEST

Look for the best in each other, and always do your best to bring it out.

1 THESSALONIANS 5:15 MSG

Friends are special gifts from God. The Bible says that friends encourage and support us.

You can be a good friend by encouraging others when they are doing something difficult and congratulating them when they do something exciting. Sometimes our friends make mistakes, but that's OK. Nobody's perfect. Be careful not to complain or criticize, and look for ways to be kind to them. When you love your friends like God asks, you bring out your best too!

THOUGHT OF THE DAY
Today, tell a friend something you like about him or her!

PRAY TODAY
Dear God, thank You for friends! Help me remember to always look for the best in others. Amen.

LAUGH TOGETHER

How we laughed and sang for joy. And the other nations said, "What amazing things the Lord has done for them."

PSALM 126:2 TLB

What makes you laugh? Do you like to tell jokes or sing silly songs? What about making funny faces? Laughing is so much fun, and it can make any day bright!

God wants us to be so happy that we laugh a lot! Laughing is a gift we can all enjoy. Laughing at someone instead of with them is not a good kind of laughter. Laughter is best when no one is hurt by it and it makes our hearts happy.

THOUGHT OF THE DAY

Larry loves to laugh and be silly! What silly things make you laugh?

PRAY TODAY

Dear God, I love to laugh! Help me share laughter with my friends and family today. Amen.

GOOD FRIENDS

Be kind to each other, tenderhearted, forgiving one another, just as God through Christ has forgiven you.

EPHESIANS 4:32 NLT

Jesus showed us what it means to be a true friend. He always told the truth. He forgave His friends when they messed up. And no matter what, He was kind to everyone.

If you want to know how to be a good friend, just look at Jesus! When you play with your friends, think about what Jesus would say or do. Try to treat people the way you think Jesus would treat them. Then you'll not only be a better friend, but you'll be shining Jesus' light for them to see!

THOUGHT OF THE DAY

How can you be a good friend today?

PRAY TODAY

Dear God, thank You for my friends. Please help me to be a good friend like You! Amen.

JUST KEEP TRYING

The Lord says, "Forget what happened before, and do not think about the past. Look at the new thing I am going to do. It is already happening. Don't you see it?"

ISAIAH 43:18–19 NCV

It can be frustrating to make mistakes. But don't worry! Jesus is the only person who ever lived a perfect life, and His sacrifice means that we can be forgiven for every mistake we make.

Ask for forgiveness, and ask God to help you learn what you need to learn. Don't ever give up! When you ask God to help you, He will be there with you! God's faithfulness and love are forever.

THOUGHT OF THE DAY

Trust in God to help you keep on learning from Him and to keep making new things happen in your heart.

PRAY TODAY

Dear God, help me to trust Your love and Your work in me. Amen.

GOD IS LOVE

We know how much God loves us, and we have put our trust in his love. God is love, and all who live in love live in God, and God lives in them.

1 JOHN 4:16 NLT

There are lots of ways to describe God, but maybe the most important one is this: God is love. Everything He does comes from that truth! When He created you, He did it out of love. When He corrects you, it's because of love. When He listens to your prayers, He covers you in love.

It doesn't matter what happens, where we go, or what we do. People can disappoint us, and we can even disappoint ourselves! But God's love is always perfect, and it's always with us. You don't ever have to worry about losing God's love.

THOUGHT OF THE DAY

Everything God does is because He loves you!

PRAY TODAY

Dear God, Your love is amazing! Thank You for loving me so perfectly. Amen.

PRAISING GOD

It is good to praise the LORD and make music to your name, O Most High.

PSALM 92:1 NIV

What is your favorite song? What kind of music do you like? One way to let God know how much we love Him is to make music and sing songs to Him. When you are happy, you can sing a happy song to God! But if you are sad, you can sing a sad song, too, and God will love hearing it just as much. Any time we make music to God, we are praising Him. And the Bible says it is good to praise the Lord!

THOUGHT OF THE DAY

What song will you sing to God today?

PRAY TODAY

Dear God, I thank You for music and for giving me songs to sing. Please help me to praise You every day. Amen.

DON'T WORRY . . . TRUST GOD

"The LORD himself will go before you. He will be with you; he will not leave you or forget you. Don't be afraid and don't worry."

DEUTERONOMY 31:8 NCV

God doesn't want you to worry about anything. Instead, He says you can trust Him to figure everything out in His perfect way!

When worry sneaks up on you, it can be hard to think of anything else. So prepare now! Think of a quick trick that will remind you to trust God. Maybe you'll say a short prayer, sing a song from church, or repeat a Bible verse about God's help. You can try memorizing the verse at the top of this page! Then next time worry comes around, you'll be ready.

THOUGHT OF THE DAY

When worry starts to creep your way, here's the best solution: pray!

PRAY TODAY

Dear God, sometimes I can't stop feeling worried. Help me remember that You've got everything under control! Amen.

WHEN YOU LOOK IN THE MIRROR

As God has said: "I will live with them and walk among them, and I will be their God, and they will be my people."

2 CORINTHIANS 6:16 NIV

How do you feel when you look in the mirror? Do you like the person you see? God sure does! He loves you, inside and out.

When you accept God's love, He sends the Holy Spirit to live in your heart every single day. You are so special that God wants to hang out with you all the time!

If you're tempted to compare yourself with someone else, stop! God made you just as you should be. So try to see yourself the way God sees you: lovable and wonderful, just as you are.

THOUGHT OF THE DAY

Next time you look in the mirror, smile! You're an amazing creation!

PRAY TODAY

Dear God, thank You for making me unique and loving me so much. Help me love myself too! Amen.

PROTECTING ANGELS

For he will order his angels to protect you wherever you go.

PSALM 91:11 NLT

Angels are special beings that do special jobs for God. Once, angels brought food to Isaiah, one of God's helpers. When baby Jesus was born, angels told the shepherds where to find Him. In heaven, angels sing songs of praise to God. The Bible tells us about another very important job that angels do—they protect us! Even though you may not see angels around you, you can be sure they are there, helping and protecting you. They are one of the many ways God shows His love for you.

THOUGHT OF THE DAY
All day, all night, angels are watching over you!

PRAY TODAY
Dear God, thank You for sending angels to protect me and keep me safe. Amen.

MAGNIFY GOD!

"My soul magnifies the Lord, and my spirit has rejoiced in God my Savior."

LUKE 1:46B–47 NKJV

Have you ever used a magnifying glass? It's a special piece of glass that makes things look bigger. Even though the glass doesn't actually change the size of what you're looking at, it helps you see and understand it much better.

Your praise acts like a magnifying glass with God! Praising God doesn't change God's amazing size and power, but it helps you see Him more clearly. You'll feel His love more strongly and begin to see all the ways He has blessed you. So praise God today! Who knows what you'll discover?

THOUGHT OF THE DAY

Praising God can magnify Him for others too!

PRAY TODAY

Dear God, I love You! I want to magnify You with praise every day! Amen.

FOLLOW GOD'S DIRECTIONS

Now, Israel, listen to the laws and commands I will teach you. Obey them so that you will live.

DEUTERONOMY 4:1 NCV

Do you know the story of Jonah? God asked him to go to a town called Nineveh and tell everyone there to follow God. But Jonah didn't want to go, so he tried to run away. He even jumped into the sea, but God sent a big fish to bring him to dry land! Finally, Jonah decided to obey God. He went to Nineveh, said what God told him to say, and everyone decided to follow God. Jonah saved a whole town that day!

When it's hard to obey God, remember Jonah's story. God's ways are always best!

THOUGHT OF THE DAY

It's always best to obey God the first time He asks!

PRAY TODAY

Dear God, help me to obey Your directions. I trust that You will be with me! Amen.

ONE BIG HAPPY FAMILY

His unchanging plan has always been to adopt us into his own family by sending Jesus Christ to die for us. And he did this because he wanted to!

EPHESIANS 1:5 TLB

God loves families! Every family looks a little bit different because every person is a little bit different. But from the very beginning, God's plan was for us to live in loving families where everyone takes care of each other.

And God's greatest plan of all is to make each of us part of His family! He watches over us and cares for us like a wonderful mom or dad does. And He wants us to support each other like brothers and sisters too! Take a look around. Is there someone you can share God's family-love with today?

THOUGHT OF THE DAY

Families can be big or small, but God's family has room for all!

PRAY TODAY

Dear God, thank You for inviting everyone to be part of Your family! I love You. Amen.

FEAR NOT!

So we will not be afraid even if the earth shakes, or the mountains fall into the sea.

PSALM 46:2 NCV

D o you ever feel afraid? Sometimes scary things happen, but God doesn't want you to be afraid. He wants you to know that no matter what happens, He will take care of you. In fact, God thought it was so important that the words "fear not" appear 365 times in the Bible. That's once for each day of the year!

Fear will try to trick you and make you believe that bad things will happen to you, but God says don't listen to fear. Instead, choose to be brave and trust Him. God will always take care of you!

THOUGHT OF THE DAY

Fear is a bully that you can defeat with faith!

PRAY TODAY

Dear God, whenever I feel afraid, I will remember that You said to "fear not." Thank You for helping me defeat fear with faith. Amen.

THE GIFT OF GUIDES

Remember what you are taught. And listen carefully to words of knowledge.

PROVERBS 23:12 ICB

God wants us to learn good lessons. So He puts people in our lives who can share their wisdom and experience to help us make good choices.

You probably have good teachers and pastors you like. Or maybe your grandparents give you great advice. And of course, your parents have lots of lessons to teach you! Think of these people as God-given guides. The words they say and the stories they share can help you live your very best life. So pay attention! You never know what God wants you to learn next.

THOUGHT OF THE DAY

What are some good lessons your parents have taught you?

PRAY TODAY

Dear God, thank You for all the great guides in my life. Help me listen carefully and learn well! Amen.

BE GENEROUS!

"It is more blessed to give than to receive."

ACTS 20:35 ESV

It's fun to get gifts or hear kind words. But it's also fun to give those things to others. In fact, it can be even better!

When you give to others, that's called being generous. God wants us to be generous with all the good gifts He's given us. How can you be generous? Some people need help to get food or clothes, so you could donate to a food bank or a shelter. Some people need you to share friendship with them. Try inviting someone new to play with your friends. You may find that giving feels even better than getting, because it means twice as much joy!

THOUGHT OF THE DAY

Be generous with kindness today. Draw a picture to give to someone special!

PRAY TODAY

Dear God, You have given me great gifts! Help me to be generous and share them with others. Amen.

DOING WHAT'S RIGHT

He grants a treasure of common sense to the honest.
He is a shield to those who walk with integrity.

PROVERBS 2:7 NLT

Integrity is a big word that means knowing the right thing to do and doing it, even when it's hard.

Sometimes the wrong choice is so much easier. It can be difficult to tell the truth or stand up for someone who is being teased. But don't worry. God will stand with you! He'll give you good words to say, and He can comfort you if you feel nervous. When you live with integrity, people learn that they can depend on you. That is exactly the kind of friend God wants you to be!

THOUGHT OF THE DAY

Can you think of a time you chose to do the right thing? How did it make you feel?

PRAY TODAY

Dear God, You help me know what is right and what is wrong. Please help me live with integrity every day. Amen.

FORGIVENESS STARTS WITH YOU

But if we confess our sins to God, he can always be trusted to forgive us and take our sins away.

1 JOHN 1:9 CEV

We know that it's important to forgive others. But did you know it's also important to forgive yourself? It's true! Everyone makes mistakes and wrong choices. Try not to get too frustrated. The important thing is to learn from your mistakes and ask God to help you try again next time.

God doesn't expect you to be perfect. He expects you to try your best and admit when you're wrong. Remember that He loves you more than you can imagine. And He's promised to forgive you no matter what. So trust Him and forgive yourself too!

THOUGHT OF THE DAY
No one is perfect. Everyone needs God!

PRAY TODAY
Dear God, thank You for loving me so much. Help me show myself kindness and forgiveness when I make mistakes. Amen.

SPEAK FROM YOUR HEART

"The mouth speaks the things that are in the heart."

Matthew 12:34 ICB

The Bible says that when we talk, the words we speak show what is inside of us. If we are glad, we speak happy words. If we are upset, angry words come out of our mouths. And have you ever been so full of joy that you just had to sing a song?

The words we say let others know how we feel. That's why it's important to fill our minds and hearts with good things. Then whatever comes out of our mouths will be helpful and kind.

THOUGHT OF THE DAY

If you want to speak with love, put God's words into your heart.

PRAY TODAY

Dear God, please help me fill my heart with Your words so I can speak with love. Amen.

GOD'S PERFECT LOVE

For though we have never yet seen God, when we love each other God lives in us, and his love within us grows ever stronger.

1 JOHN 4:12 TLB

Do you know that God's perfect love lives in you? The Bible says God lives in all His children so that they grow up in His love.

Just as God shares His love with you, He wants you to share His love with His other children too. That's how you show you're growing up in God's perfect love. When you love other people, you show them God's love at the same time. Look around and see who might need love today. Then use kind words and deeds to let them know that God loves them too!

THOUGHT OF THE DAY

Who can you surprise with God's love today?

PRAY TODAY

Dear God, thank You for loving me so much. Please help me share Your love with others every day. Amen.

CHOOSING HOPE

Let your unfailing love surround us, LORD, for our hope is in you alone.

PSALM 33:22 NLT

God loves you, and He has big plans for you. You can be sure that's true because He says so in the Bible! But there will be days when you feel like nothing is going the way you want. Those are great times to practice hope. Hope is one of God's greatest gifts! It means being sure that God is in control, even when you can't see how everything will work out. Choose hope by choosing to trust God's promises. If it's hard to trust, ask for His help! God wants you to live hopefully and confidently. He will never let you down.

THOUGHT OF THE DAY
When you live with hope, you live with joy!

PRAY TODAY
Dear God, thank You for the gift of hope. Please help me trust Your love and guidance! Amen.

STICKY SPIDER WEBS

This is what you must do: Tell the truth to each other.

ZECHARIAH 8:16A NLT

A wise man once said that when we tell lies, it is like getting stuck in a sticky spider web. One lie leads to more lies, and soon we're all tangled up and trapped like a fly in a spider's web. But the Bible gives us good advice. God says to tell the truth to each other. When we choose to tell the truth, we never have to be worried about being trapped in a sticky web of lies. Telling the truth keeps us free. It is always the best thing to do.

THOUGHT OF THE DAY

Lies will always trap us, but the truth will make us free!

PRAY TODAY

Dear God, please help me make the right choice and always tell the truth. Amen.

WHO ARE YOU?

If we are God's children, then we will receive the blessings God has for us. We will receive these things from God together with Christ.

ROMANS 8:17 ICB

How would you answer this question: Who are you? There are lots of things you might say about who you are, but do you know what the Bible says about you? If you love Jesus, the Bible says you are God's child. That means Jesus and you are in the same family! It also means that God loves and cares for you. He always hears and answers your prayers. He watches over you and wants the best for you. Always remember that you are very special to God.

THOUGHT OF THE DAY

What are some things that are great about being in God's family?

PRAY TODAY

Dear God, I am so glad You love me enough to make me a part of Your family. Thank You for always taking care of me. Amen.

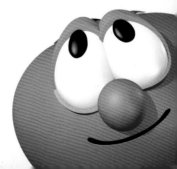

LISTEN TO WISDOM

My child, listen to what I say and remember what I command you. Listen carefully to wisdom; set your mind on understanding.

PROVERBS 2:1-2 NCV

D o you have lots to say? That's great! But don't forget to listen too!

God wants us to learn new things, so He asks us to listen to wisdom. You can do that by sitting quietly when your parents or teachers are speaking. Open your ears to hear all they say. Be sure you're not just waiting for your next chance to talk. And if you have questions, ask! When you let others speak and take time to hear their words, you can learn all kinds of things.

THOUGHT OF THE DAY

Wisdom is everywhere! Instead of hopping up right after dinner, stick around and listen to the conversation!

PRAY TODAY

Dear God, sometimes it's hard to listen when I want to talk! Please give me patience and help me hear wisdom. Amen.

GROW GOOD FRUIT

But the fruit of the Spirit is love, joy, peace, patience, kindness, goodness, faithfulness, gentleness, self-control; against such things there is no law.

GALATIANS 5:22–23 ESV

Where do apples, peaches, and pears come from? They all grow on trees! The Bible says that we are like trees, and the way we act is like the fruit we grow.

When we decide to follow Jesus, the Holy Spirit comes to live inside our hearts and makes us strong. He helps us make very special kinds of fruit, like love and joy. We speak kind words and show goodness to others. We are able to be patient and control our tempers. Because the Spirit lives in us, He helps us grow good fruit that blesses others!

THOUGHT OF THE DAY

What kind of fruit will you grow today?

PRAY TODAY

Dear God, thank You for changing me on the inside and helping me grow the good fruit of the Spirit. Amen.

BE A FRIEND!

Greater love has no one than this, that someone lay down his life for his friends.

JOHN 15:13 ESV

How can you keep good friends for a long time? The same way you make friends to begin with! Be a friend first.

The very best friends make sure to take care of each other. They listen carefully and pay attention to how the other person feels. They take turns choosing games and going first. And they work together when something is hard! Most important, good friends don't expect anything in return for doing nice things. They just enjoy doing nice things! So treat your friends the way you want to be treated. You'll always have a friend if you are one!

THOUGHT OF THE DAY

What can you do for a friend this week?

PRAY TODAY

Dear God, help me to be a great friend today and every day! Amen.

PRAY ABOUT EVERYTHING

Do not worry about anything, but pray and ask God for everything you need, always giving thanks.

PHILIPPIANS 4:6 NCV

Have you ever gotten a letter or a card in the mail? It's exciting! That's how God feels every time you pray. He loves to hear from you!

You don't have to wait until you need help with something to pray. Pray all the time! Tell God about your day, your family, and your friends. Tell Him what you're thinking about or tell Him something that happened today. God wants to spend time with you, and the more you talk to Him, the more you'll find things to say. After all, He is your best friend!

THOUGHT OF THE DAY

Tell God all about your day. He can't wait to hear from you!

PRAY TODAY

Dear God, I know You want to hear from me. Help me remember to pray all through my day. Amen.

KEEP ON KEEPING ON

But endurance must do its complete work, so that you may be mature and complete, lacking nothing.

JAMES 1:4 HCSB

When you keep on working and don't give up, that is called *endurance*. You need endurance if you want to learn to do something well, like play a sport or an instrument. But the Bible tells us that faith takes endurance too!

Each time you choose to do what God says, your faith gets a little stronger. A strong faith will help you choose God's way again and again, even when it's hard. You can also build faith-endurance by talking to God. God will help you, and He loves to hear from you! The more you follow God, the more your faith will grow.

THOUGHT OF THE DAY

Endurance takes practice. If you make a mistake, try again!

PRAY TODAY

Dear God, help me to keep on keeping on. I want to have a faith that endures, no matter what. Amen.

LISTEN UP!

My dear brothers and sisters, always be willing to listen and slow to speak.

JAMES 1:19 NCV

Talking is fun. But so is listening! Listening is how you learn new things and make new friends.

When your parents and teachers talk to you, listen closely! They have lots of wisdom and great stories to tell. What they say may even keep you safe! And be sure to listen to your friends too. Great friends are good at talking *and* listening.

Sometimes it's hard to wait for someone to finish before you start talking, but you can do it. Practice listening closely to what someone says before you respond. It might even change what you have to say!

THOUGHT OF THE DAY

Listen first, talk second.

PRAY TODAY

Dear God, help me remember to listen when others are talking. I want to learn new things and be a good friend! Amen.

GOD DOES THE IMPOSSIBLE

Jesus looked at them and said, "For people this is impossible, but for God all things are possible."

MATTHEW 19:26 NCV

God is perfect. But people aren't! We all sin—disobey God—but God says we can still be part of His family and live with Him in heaven someday. How is that possible?

It's possible because God can do anything! He sent Jesus to save us from our sin. No one else could do that! So now you don't have to worry about being good enough or doing everything perfectly. All you have to do is trust that Jesus saved you, and He will make you part of His family forever!

THOUGHT OF THE DAY
Jesus makes the impossible possible!

PRAY TODAY
Dear God, Your love is amazing! Please help me trust what You can do for me. Amen.

A SPECIAL PROMISE

"Honor your father and mother. Then you will live a long, full life in the land the LORD your God is giving you."

EXODUS 20:12 NLT

God gave some special rules to Moses. We call them the Ten Commandments. One of these commandments has a special promise attached. Read the verse above, and see if you can tell what it is.

The promise says that if you honor your father and mother, then God will bless you with a good life. But what does it mean to honor your parents? It means to show them respect, listen to them, and do what they say. It also means to show them love and kindness. When you do these things, your life is better and your family is happier too!

THOUGHT OF THE DAY

What are some ways you can honor your mom and dad today?

PRAY TODAY

Dear God, thank You for my parents. Please show me how I can honor them every day. Amen.

GOD ALWAYS FORGIVES

If we tell Him our sins, He is faithful and we can depend on Him to forgive us of our sins. He will make our lives clean from all sin.

1 JOHN 1:9 NLV

D o you ever have one of those days (or weeks!) where you feel like you keep getting in trouble? Sometimes it's hard to make good choices! But here's some good news: God never gets tired of forgiving you. Whenever we tell God our sins and ask Him to forgive us, He does it right away. It's a wonderful promise!

Remember that no one is perfect. But God's love for you will never change. He is always with you and always ready to forgive!

THOUGHT OF THE DAY
Every day is a fresh new start!

PRAY TODAY
Dear God, thank You for promising to forgive me every time I ask. Help me make better choices tomorrow. Amen.

DON'T FORGET THE TRUTH

Don't ever forget kindness and truth. Wear them like a necklace. Write them on your heart as if on a tablet.

PROVERBS 3:3 NCV

Can you think of a time when it was hard to tell the truth? Maybe you felt embarrassed, or you were afraid you'd get in trouble. But God tells us that telling the truth with kindness is always the right choice. So how do we do that when it's hard? We make sure we're always ready!

The Bible says to carry the truth around all the time. When you're honest about little things, it'll be easier to be honest about big things too. So don't forget to bring truth and kindness with you wherever you go!

THOUGHT OF THE DAY

Truth and kindness are best friends.

PRAY TODAY

Dear God, please help me tell the truth with kindness everywhere I go. Amen.

WHAT'S GOOD FOR YOU

I can do anything I want to if Christ has not said no, but some of these things aren't good for me.

1 CORINTHIANS 6:12A TLB

Habits are things you do all the time. Some habits help you, but some can hurt. How can you know which is which?

Remember that the Bible tells us that we should only do things that are kind to others and ourselves. Think of what you do each day. Maybe you pray before meals. That's a good habit! It brings you closer to God. Do you bite your nails or suck your thumb? Those aren't good habits because they can harm your body. Habits are hard to change, but God can help you choose what's good for you!

THOUGHT OF THE DAY

To start a new good habit, do it at the same time every day.

PRAY TODAY

Dear God, please show me which habits are good and which need to change. I can do anything with Your help! Amen.

GOD LIKES YOU

For the LORD your God has arrived to live among you. He is a mighty savior. He will rejoice over you with great gladness. With his love, he will calm all your fears. He will exult over you by singing a happy song.

ZEPHANIAH 3:17 NLT

Who is someone you love to spend time with? Your mom and dad? A special aunt? A best friend? Think of how you feel about that person—that's how God feels about you! God thinks you are super cool, and He really enjoys hanging out with you. Your ideas are interesting to Him. He loves to hear your questions, and your stories make Him smile. The Bible says He likes you so much, He even sings happy songs about you! Nothing makes God happier than spending time with a great friend: you!

THOUGHT OF THE DAY

What's something you and your friends talk about? Share it with God too!

PRAY TODAY

Dear God, I'm so glad we're friends! Thank You for loving and liking me so much! Amen.

BE A HERO

Now if you really obey the LORD . . . God will set you high above all nations on earth.

DEUTERONOMY 28:1 CEB

Who are your favorite Bible heroes? Larry loves the story of Joshua, who trusted some pretty weird instructions from God and won a huge battle! Pa Grape likes the story of Esther, an ordinary girl who became queen and risked her life to save her people.

All Bible heroes have one thing in common: they obeyed God. When you obey God, He promises to bless you. And His blessings may surprise you! You might not become a queen or a famous soldier, but you'll be a hero for God!

THOUGHT OF THE DAY

How can you obey God today?

PRAY TODAY

Dear God, please help me obey You, even when it's hard. I want to be a hero for You! Amen.

HELPING HANDS

Never walk away from someone who deserves help; your hand is God's hand for that person.

PROVERBS 3:27 MSG

Look at your hands. Notice anything special about them? Well, when you help others, your hands become God's hands!

Your hands can do so many things. They can draw a picture for a relative who lives far away. They can lift up a friend who's fallen down. They can give big hugs to celebrate big wins! And they can hold someone else's hand to offer a little extra support and strength. With God by your side, you can make a difference to someone—or lots of someones! What will your hands do today?

THOUGHT OF THE DAY

Jesus blesses little hands that lovingly fulfill His plans.

PRAY TODAY

Dear God, I'm so glad my little hands can do big things! Please show me how I can help someone today. Amen.

GOD'S VERY OWN

Long ago, even before he made the world, God chose us to be his very own through what Christ would do for us. . . . And he did this because he wanted to!

EPHESIANS 1:4-5 TLB

God knows you better than anyone else. He understands all of your feelings and thoughts. And He loves you like crazy.

The Bible tells us that even before God made the world, He chose us to be His own. He knew way back then that you were someone He wanted in His family. And His feelings haven't changed! He delights in you. Nothing you have done or will ever do will make God love you less. You're His child, now and forever!

THOUGHT OF THE DAY

Don't try to be anyone but you. That's who God loves!

PRAY TODAY

Dear God, thank You for making me Your very own child. I love You! Amen.

GOD'S THOUGHTS

Let God change the way you think. Then you will know how to do everything that is good and pleasing to him.

ROMANS 12:2 CEV

It's sometimes hard to make the right choice—especially if everyone around you is doing something different. But God can help!

Ask God to help you focus on things that please Him. We know He loves words that help instead of hurt. He's happy when we share what we have with others. He sees good in everyone. When you fix your mind on what is important to God, He can help you make hard decisions. You may be the only one who chooses what God wants, but that's just fine. Who knows? Others might even follow your lead!

THOUGHT OF THE DAY

Good thoughts lead to good actions!

PRAY TODAY

Dear God, please help me to be strong and make the right choice, even if it feels like I'm the only one! Amen.

SPECIAL GIFTS

Something from the Spirit can be seen in each person, to help everyone.

1 CORINTHIANS 12:7 ICB

God has given each of us special gifts. And they're all different! What's even cooler is that each gift can be used to help other people. If you love to draw, you can make pretty cards for a sick friend. If you're great at sports, you can help other kids learn how to play. If you love books, why not read to a younger sibling? Do you love animals? Offer to walk your neighbor's dog! Your gifts are wonderful. Share them with the world!

THOUGHT OF THE DAY

What's something you love to do?

PRAY TODAY

Dear God, thank You for all the things I love to do. Help me use my gifts to help others! Amen.

A FOREVER HOME

But it is just as the Scriptures say, "What God has planned for people who love him is more than eyes have seen or ears have heard. It has never even entered our minds!"

1 CORINTHIANS 2:9 CEV

Have you ever wondered about heaven? We cannot see heaven now, but we can learn some things about it from the Bible. We know it is a beautiful place God created for His children. We know that there is no pain, suffering, sickness, or even crying in heaven. We also know that it is filled with joy and light. Think of the most wonderful things you can imagine. The Bible says heaven is even better than that! One day, everyone who believes in God will have a home with Him in heaven forever!

THOUGHT OF THE DAY

Heaven is a wonderful place filled with God's glory and grace!

PRAY TODAY

Dear God, thank You for making heaven so I can have a home with You forever. Amen.

WANT OR NEED

"So don't worry at all about having enough food and clothing. . . . But your heavenly Father already knows perfectly well that you need them, and he will give them to you if you give him first place in your life and live as he wants you to."

MATTHEW 6:31–33 TLB

God knows everything about you. He knows your favorite color, your best friend, and your biggest dreams. He knows everything you want! But more importantly, He knows exactly what you need.

When you put God first, He promises to give you the things you need to live the life He's planned for you. So don't worry about having the newest books or the biggest toys. Instead, try to follow God the very best you can. God knows what you need, and He will always take care of you!

THOUGHT OF THE DAY

Think of something you want and something you need. How are they different?

PRAY TODAY

Dear God, sometimes I worry because I don't have all the things I want. Help me remember that You will give me everything I need. Amen.

SNEAK ATTACK!

Two are better than one, because they get more done by working together.

ECCLESIASTES 4:9 NCV

God loves for you to obey your parents and help others when they ask you to. But He's *really* happy when you help *without* being asked! Can you do that?

Think of it like sneak-attack helping. Maybe your mom is extra busy with work one night. Sneak attack! You can set the table for dinner. Maybe your little brother gets frustrated tying his shoes. Sneak attack! You can teach him. Maybe your friend has to finish her chores before she can play. Sneak attack! Share the chores, and start playing sooner! Sneak-attack helpfulness makes everyone's day better.

THOUGHT OF THE DAY

Everyone needs a hand sometimes. Where will your next sneak attack be?

PRAY TODAY

Dear God, please show me ways I can be helpful every day—even before someone asks! Amen.

LOTS OF LAUGHTER

He will once again fill your mouth with laughter and your lips with shouts of joy.

JOB 8:21 NLT

D o you ever get the giggles? What funny things make you laugh? God loves to hear His children enjoying life, laughing hard, and even singing silly songs! It's good to find things to be happy about. Playing with friends, splashing in puddles, making up dances, and jumping for joy are all ways to show that you're happy. Learn to look for the happy things in life and remember to help others be happy too!

THOUGHT OF THE DAY

What's your favorite joke or silly song?

PRAY TODAY

Dear God, thanks for giving me so much to be happy about! Help me share a smile with everyone I see today. Amen.

TURN ON THE LIGHTS!

Walk as children of light (for the fruit of light is found in all that is good and right and true).

EPHESIANS 5:8B–9 ESV

Have you ever seen Christmas lights on a house? At night, the tiny lights shine brightly for everyone to see. It's hard not to feel joyful around Christmas lights!

Having Jesus in your heart is like having Christmas lights up all the time! Jesus can fill your heart with joy and peace, no matter what happens. And He shows you how to make good choices so you can be a great friend and help others. So when you walk through your day, remember to turn on your lights! You'll share joy with everyone you meet.

THOUGHT OF THE DAY

Others may want to know how they can shine brightly too. Tell them that it's all from Jesus!

PRAY TODAY

Dear God, thank You that Jesus can live in my heart and light me up from the inside out! Amen.

IT'S NOT ABOUT STUFF!

Then Jesus said to them, "Be careful and guard against all kinds of greed. A man's life is not measured by the many things he owns."

LUKE 12:15 ICB

Do you ever feel like you can't stop thinking about something you want? Sometimes we can think so much about what we want that we stop thinking about what we have or even caring about our families, friends, and the people around us.

The next time you're thinking about the things you want, say thanks for everything you have instead. Then start looking for ways to spend more time with your family, friends, and—most of all—God!

THOUGHT OF THE DAY

Your relationship with God is the best thing you'll ever have.

PRAY TODAY

Dear God, help me want the same things You want for me. I'm so thankful to know You! Amen.

CREATIVE KINDNESS

Finally, all of you, be like-minded, be sympathetic, love one another, be compassionate and humble.

1 PETER 3:8 NIV

God gave you a wonderful creative mind. You can use your imagination to make-believe with your friends or draw beautiful pictures. And guess how else you can practice creativity? Being kind!

Look for nice things you can do for the people around you. Can you pick up trash that someone left at the park? Rake your neighbor's leaves? Make up a silly song to cheer up a friend? Help your parents make dinner? There are so many ways to be kind. Ask God to show you a new way today!

THOUGHT OF THE DAY

How did someone show you kindness today?

PRAY TODAY

Dear God, thank You for my imagination! Please help me think of new ways to be kind every day. Amen.

UNCONDITIONAL LOVE

And so we know the love that God has for us, and we trust that love. God is love.

1 JOHN 4:16 ICB

People often use a special word to describe God's love: unconditional. That means we don't have to do anything to get His love. It's already there. We don't have to say or do the right thing all the time. We can make mistakes and try again. Nothing will ever make God stop loving us.

God loves you just the way you are, and He loves to spend time with you! So share your thoughts and feelings with God every day. He is full of love and ready to listen to you.

THOUGHT OF THE DAY

God has always loved you, and He always will.

PRAY TODAY

Dear God, thank You for loving me all the time, no matter what! I love You too. Amen.

HAVE COURAGE

Wait for the LORD; be strong, and let your heart take courage; wait for the LORD!

PSALM 27:14 ESV

The Bible is full of courageous heroes. Queen Esther risked her life to save her people from an evil man. David the shepherd boy fought a giant and won. Gideon led 300 soldiers carrying only horns and lamps, and they defeated an army of 135,000!

You might think that brave people never feel scared. But that's not true! Courage doesn't mean you don't have any fear. You show courage when you do something *even though* you feel afraid because you know God is with you! When you trust God, He will give you courage.

THOUGHT OF THE DAY

When you feel scared, pray and wait for God's courage!

PRAY TODAY

Dear God, please help me to be brave even when I feel afraid. I'm so glad You're always by my side! Amen.

LOOK ON THE BRIGHT SIDE

A happy heart makes the face cheerful, but heartache crushes the spirit.

PROVERBS 15:13 NIV

Have you ever had a day when everything was going great? How about a day when everything seemed to go wrong? The Bible says that if we have a happy heart, we can enjoy life—even when our day isn't going the way we want.

If the rain spoils your picnic, you can splash in the puddles! What if your friend can't come over to play? Maybe you can make up a new game with your toys. Instead of getting angry when things go wrong, find something to be glad about. That's called looking on the bright side!

THOUGHT OF THE DAY

How can you look on the bright side the next time things don't go the way you want?

PRAY TODAY

Dear God, I know bad things happen sometimes. When they do, please help me to look on the bright side. Amen.

LOST AND FOUND

"What man among you, who has 100 sheep and loses one of them, does not leave the 99 in the open field and go after the lost one until he finds it?"

LUKE 15:4 HCSB

Have you ever lost something really special? You probably looked for it everywhere! It's hard to think about anything else until you have that special thing back.

That's how Jesus feels about you. You are so precious to Him that He isn't satisfied until you are safe and close to Him. He'll never get tired of chasing after you, no matter where you go. Whenever you turn to Him and accept His love, He is ready to welcome you back! No one can fill your place. You are special and important to God.

THOUGHT OF THE DAY

If ever you feel that you're lost and alone, hold on to Jesus—He'll carry you home!

PRAY TODAY

Dear Jesus, I am so glad You love me and will never leave me. I love You too! Amen.

BE WISE, ACT WISELY

Are there those among you who are truly wise and understanding? Then they should show it by living right and doing good things with a gentleness that comes from wisdom.

JAMES 3:13 NCV

I f you want to be wise, you can start by being a good listener. Pay attention when your parents and teachers speak to you. Ask lots of questions if you don't understand something. Learn Bible stories that show you what God is like.

But don't forget to act on what you learn! Wisdom doesn't mean being smarter than everyone. Wisdom means using what you've learned to follow God's rules and show love to everyone. Wise people also understand that they don't know everything, but God does. So ask God for the wisdom you need. He will give it to you!

THOUGHT OF THE DAY
True wisdom comes from following God every day!

PRAY TODAY
Dear God, help me learn more about You so I can make wise choices! Amen.

THE BEST SURPRISE

"I say to you who are listening to me, love your enemies. Do good to those who hate you. Ask God to bless those who say bad things to you. Pray for those who are cruel to you."

LUKE 6:27–28 ICB

Jesus was always surprising people. He was nice to people no one else liked. He did wonderful miracles! But one of His biggest surprises was something He said: love your enemies.

You can't always control how people treat you. But you *can* choose how you respond. If people are mean to you, they might expect you to be mean in return. But you can surprise them, just like Jesus did! Choose kind words and actions instead. You can even pray for them and ask Jesus to help you forgive them! Kindness and forgiveness are the best surprises.

THOUGHT OF THE DAY

Whom can you surprise with kindness and forgiveness today?

PRAY TODAY

Dear God, sometimes it's so hard to be kind when others aren't. Please help me always remember to love and forgive. Amen.

A GREAT LIFE

I came that they may have and enjoy life, and have it in abundance [to the full, till it overflows].

JOHN 10:10B AMP

Jesus tells us He wants us to enjoy a full life. That's great news! It means He has wonderful plans for you. You may not know what His plans are yet, but start by living a full life today! Love your family and friends the best you can. Look for ways to show others what it feels like to be loved by God. Find a way to be joyful in every task—even your chores and homework! If your life overflows with joy, you'll be ready for all God has planned for you.

THOUGHT OF THE DAY

How can you find joy in everyday things?

PRAY TODAY

Dear God, I know You want me to have a full life. Help me find joy everywhere! Amen.

CHOOSE GOD'S WAY

"Do everything the LORD your God requires. Live the way he wants you to. Obey his orders and commands."

1 KINGS 2:3A NIRV

King David gave his son Solomon some very good advice: obey God all the time. King David knew that it's not always easy to do what God says, but it's always the right choice.

We all have to make choices. Should you share or be selfish? Should you say kind words or hurting words? Should you obey your parents or just do whatever you want? Whenever you have to make a choice, stop and think: What would Jesus do? Then do that! God will be happy you listened to Him.

THOUGHT OF THE DAY

You can choose what's right today. Just follow Jesus and obey!

PRAY TODAY

Dear God, help me make choices that make You happy. I want to follow Jesus every day. Amen.

NEW FRIENDS ARE EVERYWHERE!

When you're kind to others, you help yourself; when you're cruel to others, you hurt yourself.

PROVERBS 11:17 MSG

Do you want to make new friends? Good news! New friends are everywhere! All you have to do is be kind. You can share what you have, invite someone new to play a game, and say encouraging words. Kindness is the best way to make new friends.

If someone starts at a new school or moves to a new neighborhood, making friends can seem like a big job. Ask God to show you ways to be kind to the new kids you meet. When you are friendly to others, they'll almost always want to act the same way!

THOUGHT OF THE DAY
The best way to make a friend is to be a friend!

PRAY TODAY
Dear God, I don't always know how to make new friends. Please help me start with kindness! Amen.

SAY NO TO GOSSIP

Without wood, a fire will go out, and without gossip, quarreling will stop.

PROVERBS 26:20 NCV

Have you ever met someone who likes to say mean things about others? Maybe they want you to do the same thing. But don't do it! It's called *gossip*, and it can hurt people. Instead, always choose to say good things about others—even when they aren't around.

You might feel tempted to gossip because you think people will like you more. But those aren't the kinds of friendships God wants you to have. Spreading unkind words—true or untrue—can really hurt feelings. If someone asks you to tell a secret or complain about someone, just say no. Then say something kind instead!

THOUGHT OF THE DAY

Never say anything about someone that you wouldn't tell them face to face!

PRAY TODAY

Dear God, please help me choose encouraging words instead of gossip. And help me make friends who do the same! Amen.

BEST FRIEND FOREVER

And I am convinced that nothing can ever separate us from God's love. . . . No power in the sky above or in the earth below—indeed, nothing in all creation will ever be able to separate us from the love of God that is revealed in Christ Jesus our Lord.

ROMANS 8:38–39 NLT

D o you know how much God loves you? He loves you wherever you are, however you feel, and whatever happens to you. God will never stop loving you. He is your best friend forever!

You can get an idea of God's love by reading the story of Jesus in the Bible. Jesus left His perfect home in heaven to be with you and me. And because He died for us, we get to share His perfect home forever if we ask Him. So if you haven't asked God to be your friend yet, why not do it today?

THOUGHT OF THE DAY

The Bible is full of stories of God's love. Can you think of one?

PRAY TODAY

Dear God, thank You for loving me so much and being my best friend forever! Amen.

ALWAYS THANKFUL

Give thanks in everything, for this is God's will for you in Christ Jesus.

1 THESSALONIANS 5:18 HCSB

Sometimes you may not feel very thankful. But when you give thanks in everything, you start to find good everywhere. And that means you start to find *God* everywhere!

Is it raining outside? Give thanks that God is giving the flowers plenty to drink. Your friend can't come over today? Give thanks to God for the time to invent a brand-new game to play. There's a way to be thankful in every situation. When you look closely, God can show you His love in surprising places!

THOUGHT OF THE DAY
What can you give thanks for today?

PRAY TODAY
Dear God, thank You for everything! Help me find things to be thankful for all day. Amen.

GOD MAKES YOU STRONG

We say they are happy because they did not give up.

JAMES 5:11A NCV

Have you ever done something really hard? It takes a lot of work to learn a new skill or finish a big job or even make new friends! And sometimes you might get tired and feel like giving up.

Hang in there! God can make you strong enough to do anything. Ask for His help and watch what He does. He can give you new ideas and fresh courage. He can even bring along people to help you! Nothing is too hard for God! With Him by your side, you can do anything.

THOUGHT OF THE DAY

What's something that you need to do? Ask God—He loves helping you!

PRAY TODAY

Dear God, sometimes I feel too tired to finish what I started. Please make me strong and help me do great things! Amen.

PRACTICE THE TRUTH

We are part of the same body. Stop lying and start telling each other the truth.

EPHESIANS 4:25 CEV

How do you get better at playing an instrument? You practice! In fact, it would be silly to walk into a recital and expect to play well if you hadn't been practicing.

Honesty is the same way. When you practice often, you're always ready to perform! If you aren't used to telling the truth, you can slip into telling big lies. Big lies can hurt feelings and cause trouble. But when you tell the truth all the time—even about small things—it's easier not to lie when big things come along. That's well worth putting in the practice time!

THOUGHT OF THE DAY

Tell the truth, and you will see, each time comes more easily!

PRAY TODAY

Dear God, please help me tell the truth all the time. I want to be someone people can trust! Amen.

ALWAYS AROUND

Rejoice always! Pray constantly. Give thanks in everything, for this is God's will for you in Christ Jesus.

1 Thessalonians 5:16–18 hcsb

God is always ready and waiting to hear from you. And you can talk to Him about anything! Are you having a hard day? Tell Him why, and ask for His help. Are you excited about a new friend or a fun party? Celebrate with Him! Are you nervous about a big soccer game? Ask for His peace. Do you love your family and friends? Thank God for His wonderful gifts! God is your very best friend, and He can't wait to hear what's on your mind.

THOUGHT OF THE DAY
Start each day with a "Good Morning" prayer!

PRAY TODAY
Dear God, thank You for always being around. I love knowing I can talk to You about anything! Amen.

FOLLOW THE LEADER

"Teacher, I will follow you wherever you go."

MATTHEW 8:19 ESV

Have you ever played follow-the-leader? It's a game where one person does an action while everyone else watches closely and does the very same thing.

In life, Jesus is our Leader! He asks us to watch Him closely so that we know the right way to act. Anytime you're not sure what to do, try thinking about what Jesus would do. Would Jesus share something with a friend? What kinds of words would Jesus say to others? Then all you have to do is follow the Leader!

THOUGHT OF THE DAY

Let Jesus take the lead!

PRAY TODAY

Dear Jesus, thank You for being my Leader. Help me to follow You always. Amen.

GOD CAN DO ANYTHING

Jesus looked at them intently, then said, "Without God, it is utterly impossible. But with God everything is possible."

MARK 10:27 TLB

The Bible is full of stories about people who did amazing things with God's help. Noah built a boat big enough for every kind of animal in the world. Esther convinced a powerful king to save her people. Peter walked on water! Nothing is too hard for God.

The same is true today. If you are working on something hard or you don't know how to solve a big problem, ask God to help you. You might think it's impossible, but God can do anything. So don't be shy! Ask for God's help, and He might surprise you with His answer.

THOUGHT OF THE DAY

What can you ask God to help you with today?

PRAY TODAY

Dear God, thank You that You can do anything. Please help me trust You with everything, big and small! Amen.

LIGHT IS BIGGER THAN DARKNESS

Then Jesus spoke to them again, saying, "I am the light of the world. He who follows Me shall not walk in darkness, but have the light of life."

JOHN 8:12 NKJV

It's hard to see anything in a dark room. But flip on a light switch, and BANG! Suddenly everything is clear!

Things like worry, fear, and confusion act like darkness in our lives. It's hard to see beyond them. But the Bible tells us that Jesus is a light. So following Jesus is like flipping on a giant light switch! We can give Jesus all our worries. We can feel less afraid because He is stronger than everything! He can even help us understand new things when we get confused or lost. Jesus' light makes everything clearer.

THOUGHT OF THE DAY

Every day is brighter with Jesus in it.

PRAY TODAY

Dear God, thank You for sending Jesus to light up the world! Amen.

WHAT WOULD JESUS DO?

Follow God's example, therefore, as dearly loved children.

EPHESIANS 5:1 NIV

None of us can be perfect like God. But we can all try to follow His example! One way to do this is to ask, "What would Jesus do?"

Jesus came to the world to show us how to live. He loved His mom and dad. He made good friends. He helped all sorts of people, and He was kind to everyone. He also didn't stay quiet when others were unkind—He stood up for what He knew was right. And most of all, He shared God's love with everyone. Jesus is the best example to follow!

THOUGHT OF THE DAY

If ever you don't have a clue, try asking, "What would Jesus do?"

PRAY TODAY

Dear God, thank You for sending Jesus! Help me do the things that He would do. Amen.

SHARING BLESSINGS

Every good gift and every perfect gift is from above, and comes down from the Father of lights.

JAMES 1:17 NKJV

The good things in your life are called blessings. Your family, friends, talents, even your favorite things—these are all blessings God has given you. But God doesn't want you to keep them all to yourself. He wants you to share!

If you know someone who seems lonely, invite him or her to be your friend. Ask your parents if you can have a friend over for dinner sometime. Give away some of your toys to kids who don't have very much. Sharing what God gave you is the best way to thank Him!

THOUGHT OF THE DAY

When you share God's blessings, they double!

PRAY TODAY

Dear God, thank You for all the blessings in my life! Please show me how I can share them with others. Amen.

HEAR AND DO

But be doers of the word and not hearers only.

JAMES 1:22A HCSB

Bible stories are pretty exciting! The Bible is full of interesting people, big adventures, and important lessons. It's so good to spend time hearing God's Word. But don't stop there!

God wants you to take what you know from the Bible and do something with it! Obey Jesus' directions to love everyone. Follow Ruth's example to work hard and help others. Listen to the story of the good Samaritan, and choose to be kind to people who are different from you. Don't just hear the Bible—do what it says!

THOUGHT OF THE DAY

What's a Bible story you love?

PRAY TODAY

Dear God, I love to listen to Bible stories. Please help me to be a doer, and not just a hearer! Amen.

UNLIMITED CHANCES

Those who hide their sins won't succeed, but those who confess and give them up will receive mercy.

PROVERBS 28:13 CEV

You probably know it's best to tell the truth. But it's not always easy! When we've done something wrong, we may want to lie or just pretend it didn't happen. But when you tell God the truth, you never have to worry. God gives you unlimited chances to try again!

God will always forgive you. Then, He can help you ask others for forgiveness too. That's the best way to heal hurt feelings and make things right again. So never be afraid of telling the truth. God's forgiveness never runs out.

THOUGHT OF THE DAY

God will never not forgive. It's His favorite gift to give!

PRAY TODAY

Dear God, I'm so glad You will always forgive me. Please help me tell the truth—to You and others— even when it's hard. Amen.

GOD'S GOOD RULES

Through the Word we are put together and shaped up for the tasks God has for us.

2 TIMOTHY 3:17 MSG

Is it hard for you to follow the rules? Some people think rules are no fun. But God gave us good rules to show us how to be happy!

God gave Moses a list of simple instructions called the Ten Commandments. It's like a treasure map to a great life! When you follow the map, you'll live happily with your family and friends, and you'll have a strong friendship with God. Nothing could be better! So when you hear God telling you what to do, praise Him. He's showing you the way to the life He's planned for you.

THOUGHT OF THE DAY

God's rules totally rule!

PRAY TODAY

Dear God, sometimes it's hard to do what You want me to. Help me remember that You want what's best for me! Amen.

TAKE GOOD CARE!

Don't you know that you are God's temple and that God's Spirit lives in you?

1 CORINTHIANS 3:16 NCV

One of God's greatest gifts is easy to see: your body! Your body lets you move around, see beautiful things, laugh big belly laughs, and enjoy yummy food. You and your body can do amazing things!

So how can you thank God for this super cool gift? Keep your body happy and healthy! Eat all kinds of good foods that help you grow. Take scrubby, bubbly baths, and brush your teeth every day. Wear a helmet when you ride your bike. You can do lots of things to care for the wonderful body God gave you!

THOUGHT OF THE DAY

What are three ways you can care for your body today?

PRAY TODAY

Dear God, thank You for giving me a body that can do so much! Help me take good care of it. Amen.

BUT FIRST, GOD!

This is the day the LORD has made; let us rejoice and be glad in it.

PSALM 118:24 ESV

What do you do when you wake up each morning? Do you brush your teeth? Wash your face? You probably eat breakfast, and I hope you get dressed! There's a lot to do once you're out of bed. But here's something you can do while you're still snuggled in your blankets: pray! Each new day is a gift from God. Thank Him for today and for all the wonderful plans He has in store for you. Ask for His help with anything you're worried about. Praise Him for His love and goodness. It's always a good idea to start your day with God!

THOUGHT OF THE DAY

Wake up and pray, "Hooray for today!"

PRAY TODAY

Dear God, thank You for each and every day You give me! I love the world You have made. Amen.

WHAT DO YOU HAVE?

Don't set your heart on anything that is your neighbor's.

EXODUS 20:17B MSG

D o you and your friends have exactly the same toys? Of course not! Sharing new things makes playing together really fun. But sometimes, you might feel upset when a friend gets something you want. When you let that bad feeling become bigger than the good feelings of playing together, that's called *jealousy*. And it's no fun for anyone! God doesn't want you to feel that way. That's why He says to remember the good things you already have! Everyone has good gifts from God. What are yours? When you're happy with what you have, you can be happy for others too!

THOUGHT OF THE DAY

If your friend gets something really cool, celebrate! Then you'll *both* be happy!

PRAY TODAY

Dear God, please help me remember the good things I have. I don't want to be jealous—I want to be happy! Amen.

GOD'S FAVORITE GIFT

"Praise the name of God forever and ever, for he has all wisdom and power."

DANIEL 2:20 NLT

What's the best gift you've ever received? Did you know that God loves to receive gifts too? But He doesn't want things like toys or games or a new bike. God's favorite gift is your praise!

Praising God means celebrating how good He is. And everyone's praise is different. Some people like to sing and dance to celebrate God, while others like to pray quietly. Often, praise is joyful! But you can also praise God when things aren't going your way. When you praise God all the time, it shows that you love Him and believe that He will care for you. And that's the only gift God wants!

THOUGHT OF THE DAY

Giving God the gift of praise keeps you peaceful all your days!

PRAY TODAY

Dear God, You are so good all the time! Help me remember to praise You when I'm happy, sad, and everything in between. Amen.

AN ENCOURAGING WORD

So encourage each other and give each other strength.

1 THESSALONIANS 5:11A NCV

D o you know someone who is going through a hard time? Maybe they feel sad or upset about changes at home or school, or they're trying to do something new and challenging. You can help! The Bible says you can make your friends stronger just by saying encouraging words!

Encouraging words are words that make someone feel better about doing something hard. You can say "You're doing great!" or "I know you can do it!" Even something as simple as "I love being your friend" can be a big help. Everyone feels stronger when they know someone cares about them. Be that someone today!

THOUGHT OF THE DAY

See if you can find someone to encourage today!

PRAY TODAY

Dear God, thank You for good friends. Please give me encouraging words to say to them! Amen.

HOW GOD SEES YOU

I will praise You because I have been remarkably and wonderfully made. Your works are wonderful, and I know this very well.

PSALM 139:14 HCSB

When we look at each other, we can see only what's outside. But when God looks at you, He sees inside your heart. He knows the things you love and the things you don't. He knows the things that make you nervous or excited or curious. He sees what makes you the uniquely wonderful kid He created. And He loves every part of you!

The book of Genesis says God made us in His image. That means you are a reflection of God! So thank Him when you look at yourself. You are a beautiful, important creation—inside and out!

THOUGHT OF THE DAY

God made only one you!

PRAY TODAY

Dear God, thank You that You see my outside and my inside. Help me remember that who I am is more important than what I look like. Amen.

MANNERS MATTER

Let everyone see that you are considerate in all you do.

PHILIPPIANS 4:5A NLT

Here's an easy way to be kind: have good manners. Does that surprise you? It's true! When you're polite, you show others that you care about their feelings. And that makes them feel great!

Look for ways to practice good manners today. After you eat, you can take your empty plate to the kitchen. If you're at a restaurant, you can play quietly in your seat until everyone is ready to go. Join in conversations, and try not to interrupt others—even when you have something really fun to say! Good manners show others that they matter to you!

THOUGHT OF THE DAY

What manners are hardest for you to remember? What are the easiest?

PRAY TODAY

Dear God, thank You for giving me such a great way to show kindness! Please help me remember my manners every day. Amen.

PATIENTLY WAITING

I waited patiently for the Lord. He turned to me and heard my cry.

PSALM 40:1 NCV

Have your parents ever told you to be patient? It's hard to wait for things we want, but we have to trust that our parents know the best time to give us things. It's the same with God!

God has big plans for you, but only He knows when those plans will happen. That means you may have to be patient. Trust that God knows the perfect moment to reveal His great plans for you, and pray that He'll use the waiting time to prepare you for what's coming!

THOUGHT OF THE DAY

Helping others is a great way to prepare for God's plans!

PRAY TODAY

Dear God, thank You for making big plans for me. Please help me wait patiently! Amen.

CELEBRATE TODAY!

This is the day that the LORD has made. Let us rejoice and be glad today!

• PSALM 118:24 NCV

Every day is a reason to celebrate! Do you know why? Because God created it! He made the sun rise, the flowers bloom, and the wind blow. He made the clouds roll by or the sun shine brightly or the thunder crash. And He made today full of special opportunities just for you.

Today may not be a special day like Christmas or your birthday, but every day has something to be excited about. Who knows who you'll meet or what you'll do? Each day you can celebrate God's awesome love for you!

THOUGHT OF THE DAY

Today is a special gift. Find a way to celebrate it!

PRAY TODAY

Dear God, thank You for today. Let's celebrate it together! Amen.

GOD IS LOOKING AFTER YOU!

The LORD is my light and my salvation; whom shall I fear? The LORD is the strength of my life; of whom shall I be afraid?

PSALM 27:1 NKJV

Do you ever feel afraid? God can help! He is bigger and more powerful than anything in the entire universe. And He will never, ever leave you! With God by your side, you can face anything.

Sometimes that's hard to remember. Fear is a feeling, and feelings can be overwhelming. But nothing is too hard for God. Try repeating a verse about God's love and power. You can memorize the one at the top of this page!

When you fill your mind with God, He'll fill your heart with courage.

THOUGHT OF THE DAY

God is always looking out for you. You have nothing to fear!

PRAY TODAY

Dear God, sometimes I get scared. Please keep my family and me safe, and help me trust You all the time. Amen.

PRACTICE LOVING

Dear friends, let us practice loving each other, for love comes from God and those who are loving and kind show that they are the children of God, and that they are getting to know him better.

1 JOHN 4:7 TLB

'll bet you already know that practice is important if you want to get better at playing a game, reading, or making music. But the Bible says we also need to practice loving each other! We can do that by thinking of ways to be kind. Sharing, taking turns, offering to help, giving a hug, and saying "please" and "thanks" are all ways to be kind. You could also surprise your mom by doing extra chores or give toys to kids who don't have very much. Look around at home and at school. Who needs some extra love today? Can you think of ways to practice loving them?

THOUGHT OF THE DAY

If you want to live God's way, practice loving every day!

PRAY TODAY

Dear God, I want to love like You love. Please help me find ways to practice loving today. Amen.

A HAPPY FACE

A glad heart makes a cheerful face.

PROVERBS 15:13 ESV

Do you know you can often tell how someone is feeling just by looking at their face? How does someone look when they're angry? How do they look when they're sad? The Bible says that when we have a glad heart, our face will look happy. But how do you make your heart glad? You can do that by remembering all the wonderful things God has done for you. Look at the world and thank Him for the beauty you see. Sing a song to Him. When you take time to be thankful to God, your heart will be glad, and you'll show it by having a happy face!

THOUGHT OF THE DAY

Give thanks to God, and in a while, your face will wear a happy smile!

PRAY TODAY

Dear God, thank You for being so kind to me and for giving me a heart filled with gladness. Amen.

LOVING CORRECTION

But don't, dear friend, resent God's discipline; don't sulk under his loving correction. It's the child he loves that God corrects; a father's delight is behind all this.

PROVERBS 3:11–12 MSG

What happens when you disobey your parents? You may have to apologize, take a time-out, or help clean or fix a mess. None of that stuff is super fun. But it's all important. Your parents love you, and they want you to make good choices. That's why they take the time to correct you when you need a little help!

God is just the same. He loves us so much that He takes time to gently correct us when we disobey Him. So try not to get upset. Ask God what you can do differently next time!

THOUGHT OF THE DAY

God's beside you day and night, showing you what's wrong and right!

PRAY TODAY

Dear God, I don't always like to be corrected. Please help me remember that it's all because You love me! Amen.

NO LIE IS A GOOD LIE

Since you put away lying, Speak the truth, each one to his neighbor, because we are members of one another.

EPHESIANS 4:25 HCSB

I t's tempting to think that a small lie doesn't matter, especially if it gets you out of trouble. But it's still unfair to the person you tell, and it could hurt someone else. The best thing to do is always tell the truth!

The Bible tells us to "put away lying" and speak honestly. Try thinking about lying as something you put away on a high shelf so you can't even reach it. That way, you can't help but tell the truth!

THOUGHT OF THE DAY

When you tell the truth about something you've done wrong, you can ask for forgiveness and move on!

PRAY TODAY

Dear God, help me to always choose the truth and put lies somewhere I can't reach them! Amen.

DON'T WORRY, KEEP PRAYING

Do not worry about anything, but pray and ask God for everything you need, always giving thanks.

PHILIPPIANS 4:6 NCV

Everyone feels worried sometimes. God wants to help! So He gives us good advice in the Bible: pray.

He even tells us how to pray! First, tell God what's worrying you and ask Him for courage and peace. Then, remember to give thanks.

Give thanks for what? For everything! Sometimes worry seems to hide the good things God's done. So look around and tell God "thank You!" for every good thing you notice. It could be as big as your mom's love or as small as a puppy snuggle. When you spend time thinking about God's good gifts, your worry will fade away!

THOUGHT OF THE DAY

How does it feel when you get worried? What's something you can always remember to be thankful for?

PRAY TODAY

Dear God, thank You for listening to me when I get worried. Help me see all the good things You've given me! Amen.

PARENTS CAN HELP

The one who lives with integrity is righteous; his children who come after him will be happy.

PROVERBS 20:7 HCSB

Your parents know a whole lot about so many things. And they want you to learn and grow into who God wants you to be! So why not ask them for their help?

You can ask them to help you with almost anything. Are you trying to get better at something? Is it hard to be kind sometimes? Do you have questions about God? They would love to help you! Even if they don't know the answer to a question, they'll figure it out with you. Parents are some of God's greatest gifts!

THOUGHT OF THE DAY

Ask your parents to tell you a story about your grandparents. You might be surprised at what you'll learn!

PRAY TODAY

Dear God, please bless my parents! Thank You that they love me and want to help me grow. Amen.

HE'S GOT THE ANSWERS!

*If you don't know what you're doing, pray to the Father.
He loves to help.*

JAMES 1:5 MSG

D o you ever feel like you don't know what to do? You're not alone! The only one who knows everything all the time is God. So why not ask Him next time?

When you're worried about a decision, you might think you've thought of everything. Maybe you have, but you should always ask God to help you too. He can help you choose, and He might even give you an idea you hadn't thought about! God loves to help you. And since He's always working for your good, you can trust that His ideas are the best ones!

THOUGHT OF THE DAY

Start your day by praying for God's help in everything you do.

PRAY TODAY

Dear God, thank You for having all the answers! Please help me choose the things You want today. Amen.

FAITH TO ACT

In the same way, faith by itself, if it is not accompanied by action, is dead.

JAMES 2:17 NIV

I f someone says they can run fast, how do you know it's true? You have to see that person actually run! It's the same with faith. The Bible tells us that just saying we trust in God is not enough. We need to *show* people that we have faith in God.

But how do we do that? We prove our faith by our actions. Being kind, sharing, and helping others are all actions that show we love God. They prove our faith is real!

THOUGHT OF THE DAY

What actions can you do today to show your faith is real?

PRAY TODAY

Dear God, please help me put my faith in action today. Amen.

LOOK FOR GOODNESS

The one who searches for what is good finds favor, but if someone looks for trouble, it will come to him.

Goodness is a funny thing. It might not be obvious, but God says if you look for goodness, you'll find it. You can find goodness in other people, at school, and in yourself.

Sometimes we can get distracted by things that worry us or make us upset. Looking for good things in any situation keeps your heart cheerful because you'll find what God wants you to see. So ask God to show you good things and the ways He might be working. They are all around you!

THOUGHT OF THE DAY

Look around you. What are three good things you see right now?

PRAY TODAY

Dear God, please show me how to find goodness everywhere. Amen.

LOVE YOUR WHOLE FAMILY

But Ruth said, "Don't beg me to leave you or to stop following you. Where you go, I will go. Where you live, I will live. Your people will be my people, and your God will be my God."

RUTH 1:16 NCV

The most important thing in any family is love. You should always show love to each person in your family. And you should always, always feel loved!

Ruth knew how to love her family well. When her husband died, she stayed with her mother-in-law, Naomi, and worked hard to take care of her. Naomi loved Ruth as well, and she cared for her by sharing wisdom and good advice. With Naomi's help, Ruth got married again, and one of her descendants was Jesus!

Everyone in a family has an important role to play. When you all look out for one another, great things can happen!

THOUGHT OF THE DAY

How does your family show love to each other?

PRAY TODAY

Dear Lord, please help me remember that loving You and my family are more important than anything! Amen.

WHEN TIMES ARE TOUGH

The LORD says, "I will rescue those who love me. I will protect those who trust in my name. When they call on me, I will answer; I will be with them in trouble."

PSALM 91:14–15 NLT

Some days it feels like nothing goes right. But don't give up! Hold on to God, and He will help you get through anything.

Whenever you feel lost or in trouble, you can always call out to God. He's promised to stay with you always, so you can be sure He'll hear your prayer! Ask for His help and comfort, and remember that hard times don't last forever. God is with you, working out His purposes in your life. He wants to make you more like Him and closer to Him through whatever hard thing you are going through.

THOUGHT OF THE DAY

Life gets hard sometimes, but God is always there to help.

PRAY TODAY

Dear God, help me turn to You when I'm having a hard day. I know You can comfort and help me! Amen.

GOD CAN HELP

Depend on the Lord and his strength. Always go to him for help.

1 CHRONICLES 16:11 ICB

D o you ever feel like you don't know what to do? Do you sometimes need an idea about how to solve a problem? The Bible says that you can depend on the Lord and His strength. That means He won't let you down. You can ask God to help you when you need answers to your problems. He loves to hear from you, and He wants to give you courage, strength, and wisdom. Even if it's a big, big problem, nothing is too hard for God. You are His precious child, and He promises to be your helper.

THOUGHT OF THE DAY

God is there to help you through whatever seems too hard to do!

PRAY TODAY

Dear God, thank You for loving me and for always being there to help me. Amen.

MAKE TODAY HAPPY

What joy for those who can live in your house, always singing your praises. What joy for those whose strength comes from the LORD.

PSALM 84:4–5 NLT

Each day is a new gift from God. That's a pretty happy thought, isn't it?

But some days, you might not feel very happy. That's OK. God can still help you find joy—which is even stronger than happiness! Remember that God is good every day, and He loves you. That never changes. Try praising God for the great things He's done. Find something—anything!—to thank Him for.

It's easy to praise God when you're feeling great. But looking for joy when you don't feel like it makes you strong in the Lord. And that's the happiest thought of all!

THOUGHT OF THE DAY

When you go looking for joy, you'll always find it!

PRAY TODAY

Dear God, thank You that Your love never changes. Help me find reasons to be happy every day! Amen.

LIVING TOGETHER

How good and how pleasant it is when God's people live together in unity!

PSALM 133:1 NIV

Who lives with you at your house? Some families are large, and some are small; but God says that it is always good when we live together in unity. Unity means that even though we are different from one another, we try to get along. Sometimes you will get your way, but sometimes someone else gets their way. Sometimes you get to do your favorite thing or have your favorite food for dinner. Sometimes it is someone else's turn to have their favorites. It isn't always easy to get along, but it makes God happy when we try.

THOUGHT OF THE DAY

What are some ways your family has fun together?

PRAY TODAY

Dear God, thank You for giving me my family. Please help me to do my part to live in unity with everyone here. Amen.

A LISTENING EAR

"Then you will call upon Me and go and pray to Me, and I will listen to you."

JEREMIAH 29:12 NKJV

Sometimes it can feel like no one hears what you say. But God is always listening!

The Bible says that whenever you talk to God, He will listen to you. He listens because He loves you so much! It doesn't matter what you talk about. You can tell Him what makes you happy or sad. You can tell Him what happened during the day or talk through a problem you're trying to solve. You can even sing Him a song! Whatever you have to say, however you want to say it, God loves to hear your voice.

THOUGHT OF THE DAY

God listens to every word. Always know that you've been heard!

PRAY TODAY

Dear God, I'm so glad You listen to my prayers. Thank You for always loving me and caring for me. Amen.

BELIEVE WHAT GOD SAYS!

Abraham trusted God, and when God told him to leave home and go far away to another land that he promised to give him, Abraham obeyed. Away he went, not even knowing where he was going.

HEBREWS 11:8 TLB

God told Abraham to go to a special land He'd prepared for Abraham and his family. But God didn't say how to get there! Still, Abraham and his wife trusted God. They knew His promises are always good, so they gathered their things and started walking. And God led them exactly where they were supposed to go!

When you do what God asks, you show that you trust Him too. Maybe He wants you to be patient with your siblings or tell someone you're sorry. It isn't always easy to do what God asks, but it's always a good idea. Just ask Abraham!

THOUGHT OF THE DAY
What is something you think God wants you to do?

PRAY TODAY
Dear God, I want to trust You like Abraham did. Please help me do the things You ask me to! Amen.

THE WAY, THE TRUTH, AND THE LIFE

Jesus answered, "I am the way and the truth and the life. No one comes to the Father except through me."

JOHN 14:6 NIV

One day, Jesus told His disciples that He is three things: the way, the truth, and the life. He is the way because He shows us the way to live. When we follow His example, we treat others kindly and make good choices. He is the truth because everything He says is true. We can always trust what Jesus says! And He is the life because when we believe in Him we can live with God in heaven forever.

Jesus is everything you need. So trust Him with everything you have!

THOUGHT OF THE DAY

Jesus always says what's true and offers all good things to you!

PRAY TODAY

Dear God, thank You for sending Jesus to show me the way, to tell me the truth about You, and to invite me to live with You forever. I love You! Amen.

TELLING THE TRUTH

You want me to be completely truthful, so teach me wisdom.

PSALM 51:6 NCV

God wants us to tell the truth. Sometimes it seems easier to lie, but pretty soon that lie will start to bother you. You will start to feel guilty, and you might even have to tell more lies to keep the truth a secret! It's much simpler, and more loving, to tell the truth right away.

The good news is that God can help you. And when you tell the truth all the time, other people learn they can trust you, and they'll want to be your friend. Telling the truth is always the best choice.

THOUGHT OF THE DAY

The truth will set you free!

PRAY TODAY

Dear God, help me to tell the truth always. Thank You for loving me no matter what! Amen.

BE A FAITHFUL FOLLOWER

I have chosen the way of faithfulness; I set your rules before me.

PSALM 119:30 ESV

Being faithful to God means choosing to follow God's rules, even if it's hard. We can show God we love Him by practicing faithfulness.

Being faithful doesn't just make God happy—it can make you happy too! God's rules are designed to give you the very best life. God tells us to be honest because He knows that's how to have great friendships. He tells us not to say mean things, because He knows that would make us and others sad. He tells us to be generous with what we have because sharing shows love. Choosing faithfulness to God means choosing happiness!

THOUGHT OF THE DAY

God's rules are like a secret code to living a great life!

PRAY TODAY

Dear God, it's not always easy to follow the rules. But I know Your rules are good! Please help me always to choose Your way. Amen.

PUT GOD FIRST

"You shall have no other gods before me."

EXODUS 20:3 ESV

Have you heard of the Ten Commandments? They are ten laws God gave to His people so they would know how to be safe and happy. The first law was to love God more than anything else.

Here's a secret: the first commandment is the key to the other nine! When you love God more than anything, you want to make Him happy. So, telling the truth, respecting your parents, and going to church are easy choices because they're things God loves. And remember that what God wants most is for you to stay close to Him. When you put Him first, that's exactly what happens!

THOUGHT OF THE DAY

Can you memorize all Ten Commandments? The first three are all about loving God!

PRAY TODAY

Dear God, thank You for telling me how to stay close to You. Help me follow Your commandments every day. Amen.

GIVING AND RECEIVING

"Give, and you will receive. Your gift will return to you in full—pressed down, shaken together, running over, and poured into your lap. The amount you give will determine the amount you get back."

LUKE 6:38 NLT

Boys and girls who share always seem to have lots of friends. Others want to play with them, and they end up having more and more fun. The Bible says that's because when we give, then we will receive. When we give away kindness and share with others, we receive kindness from others, and they want to share with us! Giving and receiving work together to bring God's blessings to everyone!

THOUGHT OF THE DAY

What will you choose to give to someone else today?

PRAY TODAY

Dear God, thank You for giving so much to me. Help me to be a good giver today. Amen.

KIND THOUGHTS

A wise person is patient. He will be honored if he ignores a wrong done against him.

PROVERBS 19:11 ICB

We know God wants us to forgive one another, but what does forgiveness really mean?

The Bible tells us that forgiving means giving up our anger and deciding not to hurt someone the way they hurt us. It's not always easy—especially if our feelings have been hurt badly—but ask for God's help! Tell God how you are feeling and ask Him to take your anger away.

When you truly forgive someone, you'll notice that you feel much happier. Your thoughts aren't angry anymore! Then you can get back to being a good friend.

THOUGHT OF THE DAY

Forgiveness sets everyone free from anger, especially you!

PRAY TODAY

Dear God, please take my angry thoughts away and help me forgive others quickly. Amen.

JUST CELEBRATE!

Celebrate God all day, every day.

PHILIPPIANS 4:4 MSG

Are you ready to party? The Bible tells us that we can celebrate every single day! That's because God is good, and He loves us no matter what. What could be better than that?

Think of all the things that make you smile! Do you have good friends? Did you have fun with your family today? Maybe the sun is shining brightly right now, or the rain is giving the garden a good drink. Every day is filled with reasons to praise God. So sing a song or jump for joy! God loves to see you celebrate!

THOUGHT OF THE DAY

How would you throw a party for God?

PRAY TODAY

Dear God, You are amazing! Help me remember to celebrate You every single day! Amen.

JOYFUL ALL THE TIME

"Don't be sad! This is a special day for the Lord, and he will make you happy and strong."

NEHEMIAH 8:10 CEV

Depending on what's going on around you, you might feel happy or sad at different times during the day. We can ask God to encourage us with His love and care, especially when we are sad. He can be strong for us. This is what it means to have the joy of the Lord. It's a special gift from God that helps you feel peaceful in every situation.

When you have joy from the Lord, you are sure that God is in control, and that keeps you from getting too worried or upset. So today, ask God for joy. He would love to give it to you!

THOUGHT OF THE DAY

The joy of the Lord can be ours no matter what is going on.

PRAY TODAY

Dear God, please give me the gift of Your joy. I want to know Your peace and share it with others! Amen.

COME BACK TO GOD

*Return to the L*ORD *your God, for he is merciful and compassionate, slow to get angry and filled with unfailing love.*

JOEL 2:13 NLT

Have you ever done or said something you wish you could take back? It happens to everyone! And it's not always easy to know what to do next.

Whenever you feel sorry or sad, talk to God. The Bible tells us that God doesn't get angry quickly and He is full of love. When you ask Him for forgiveness, He celebrates! He can't wait to gather you up in His arms and cover you with love. Then His love can give you courage to ask others for their forgiveness, too, and help make things right. There's nothing God's love can't do!

THOUGHT OF THE DAY

No matter what you do or where you go, you can always come back to God!

PRAY TODAY

Dear God, thank You for loving me so much. When I do something wrong, help me come back to You right away! Amen.

FOR SUCH A TIME AS THIS

"Who knows? Maybe you were made queen for just such a time as this."

ESTHER 4:14 MSG

Esther was a poor young woman who didn't seem very important. But one day she became queen! Soon after that, her people were in danger, and as queen, she was the only one who could convince the king to save them!

God had an important plan for Esther, but she would never have guessed it! In the same way, God has a plan for your life. You might not know what it is, but you can be sure it's very good. So trust God. His plans are even better than you can imagine!

THOUGHT OF THE DAY

You are meant to be where you are, right now. Your life is important!

PRAY TODAY

Dear God, I am so excited about Your plans for me! Please give me courage to trust You when I don't know what's coming next. Amen.

SPREAD CHEER

A cheerful heart is good medicine, but a broken spirit saps a person's strength.

PROVERBS 17:22 NLT

When you get sick, your mom or dad probably gives you medicine. Well, the Bible says that cheerfulness is like good medicine—it makes people feel better.

So how can you show cheerfulness? One way is to smile. And that can be contagious—most people will smile right back! Another way is to share kind words and deeds.

God loves it when we have a cheerful heart and share it with others. It lets them see the love and joy that God has given us.

THOUGHT OF THE DAY

Your smile can change someone's day!

PRAY TODAY

Dear God, thank You for giving me a cheerful heart and finding ways to give cheerfulness to others. Amen.

TOUGH FORGIVENESS

Never pay back evil with more evil. Do things in such a way that everyone can see you are honorable.

ROMANS 12:17 NLT

Joseph was a man in the Bible who had a tough life! His brothers sent him far away from home, and he was put in prison. But Joseph trusted God, and one day he became very powerful. He could have gotten back at his brothers, but instead, he forgave them. He even helped them when they were in trouble!

God gave Joseph the strength he needed to choose forgiveness. If someone hurts you, you may want to stay angry for a while. Don't do it! Ask God to help you let go of your anger and forgive. You'll feel a lot better!

THOUGHT OF THE DAY

Is there someone you're angry with? Ask God to help you forgive them today!

PRAY TODAY

Dear God, help me to forgive people like Joseph did. I know I will feel a lot better! Amen.

SMALL CHOICES, BIG CHANGES

Put on the new self, created to be like God in true righteousness and holiness.

EPHESIANS 4:24 NIV

D o you have habits? Some habits, like brushing your teeth or saying your prayers, are very good. But some habits can hurt you. Maybe it's easy to tell a lie, or you yell when you get angry. The good news is, God can help you change bad habits!

The Bible says that when we follow God, it's like we get a brand-new self. That means we can make brand-new choices because God is helping! And nothing is too hard for God. Just start today, and start small. One better choice every day can make a big difference.

THOUGHT OF THE DAY

What is something you'd like to do differently? How can you start today?

PRAY TODAY

Dear God, please help me make better choices every day. I want to have only good habits! Amen.

A ROYAL LAW

*If you really keep the royal law according to the Scripture,
"Love your neighbor as yourself," you are doing right.*

JAMES 2:8 NIV

How do you like to be treated? Do you want others to say kind words? Share their toys? Invite you to play with them? Guess what? That's exactly how you should treat everyone else!

The Bible calls this idea the "royal law." That sounds pretty important! When you love others the same way you love yourself, you'll make them feel like kings and queens. And the best part is, you're showing them what God's love looks like too! So always try to remember the royal law. You'll be the king of kindness!

THOUGHT OF THE DAY

The greatest way to wear a crown is spreading kindness in your town!

PRAY TODAY

Dear God, thank You for giving me such a great way to remember how to treat others. You are the real King of kindness! Amen.

HOORAY FOR TODAY!

This is the day that the LORD has made. Let us rejoice and be glad today!

PSALM 118:24 NCV

God has made each day brand-new for you! Isn't that a wonderful thought?

It's easy to get excited about days like holidays and birthdays. But God has given you lots of reasons to be thankful for every other day too. Look around! You can find God in even the most normal days. Watch how He moves the clouds across the sky. Look at the birds, who seem to know exactly which way to fly. Pay attention to the people you meet and all the things you can do! Every day is a little different. How has God made today special?

THOUGHT OF THE DAY

What are three things you can be happy about today?

PRAY TODAY

Dear God, thank You for today—and every day! Help me see You everywhere I look. Amen.

DO YOUR BEST

Let your patience show itself perfectly in what you do. Then you will be perfect and complete and will have everything you need.

JAMES 1:4 NCV

Everyone has work they need to do. Maybe you have chores at home, like cleaning your room or setting the table for dinner. Maybe you help out with a younger brother or sister. And maybe you go to school, where you are learning new things every day. Whatever you do, God wants you to do your best.

Doing your best doesn't mean being perfect. You make God happy when you take your time, try hard, and enjoy what you're doing. And when you see that you've done a good job, you'll feel happy too!

THOUGHT OF THE DAY

How can you do your best at something today?

PRAY TODAY

Dear God, please help me work hard at everything I do. I want to do good work! Amen.

A TINY SEED

"Truly I tell you, if you have faith as small as a mustard seed, you can say to this mountain, 'Move from here to there,' and it will move. Nothing will be impossible for you."

MATTHEW 17:20B NIV

Have you ever planted a seed? Seeds are usually very small. But when you plant them in good soil and give them water and sunlight, they can grow to become colorful flowers, tasty vegetables, or even huge trees!

God says that faith can grow too. Your faith can be as tiny as a seed—you don't have to know everything about God or have an answer to every question. But when you take care of your faith by reading your Bible, going to church, and praying, God will help your faith grow strong, just like a beautiful tree.

THOUGHT OF THE DAY

A tiny seed of faith can grow to do great things.

PRAY TODAY

Dear God, there is a lot I don't know, but I know I love You! Please help my seed of faith to grow big and strong. Amen.

BE A LIGHT

"Let your light shine before others, that they may see your good deeds and glorify your Father in heaven."

MATTHEW 5:16 NIV

Think about what a light does. Light helps you see clearly, find the right way to go, and maybe even feel less afraid. Those are all things Jesus does too! When you show Jesus' love to others, it's like shining a bright light for everyone. When people see that light, they'll see that you serve Jesus. And they may want to follow Him too!

Jesus depends on you to shine His light to the world. So follow His ways, be kind to others, and help people who need it. You can be Jesus' very bright light!

THOUGHT OF THE DAY

How can you shine Jesus' light at school or at home?

PRAY TODAY

Dear God, I want to be a light and show Jesus' love to everyone I meet. Please show me how I can shine bright! Amen.

A BIG JOB

"This is my command—be strong and courageous! Do not be afraid or discouraged. For the LORD your God is with you wherever you go."

JOSHUA 1:9 NLT

God had a big job for Joshua. He wanted Joshua to become the leader of His people. Joshua was nervous. He was used to following his friend Moses, and he was scared to lead by himself. But God told Joshua He would always be with him.

It's normal to feel nervous when we have a big job to do. But you don't have to be afraid! God is right there with you, and He can help you do anything. So don't walk away from new things. You might miss out on something great! Just ask God, and He will give you courage.

THOUGHT OF THE DAY

When you've got a big job to do, trust God, do your best, and see what happens!

PRAY TODAY

Dear God, thank You that You're always with me, no matter what I need to do! Amen.

KEEP BELIEVING

Immediately the father of the child cried out and said with tears, "Lord, I believe; help my unbelief!"

MARK 9:24 NKJV

D o you love to ask questions? God can handle any question you ask Him. And He never gets tired of them!

When you ask God questions, you show that you trust His wisdom. So ask away! He may not answer quickly, and His answers may not always make sense to you right away. Try not to get discouraged. Keep asking God for help and believing in His goodness. And stay curious! When you stick close to God and talk to Him often, your faith gets stronger. Then you won't miss anything He has to say.

THOUGHT OF THE DAY

Sometimes answers show up in the Bible. Ask God to help you find them!

PRAY TODAY

Dear God, when I have a lot of questions, please help me trust You to give me the answers I need. Amen.

SMALL CHOICES, BIG HERO

"This is what the LORD All-Powerful says: 'Do what is right and true. Be kind and merciful to each other.'"

ZECHARIAH 7:9 NCV

You may have heard someone called a "hero" because he or she did something big and brave. But you can be a hero by doing small things too!

God tells us that little things can help others in a big way. You can show kindness by sharing with others and speaking nice words. You can show mercy by forgiving a friend quickly or by caring for someone who is sick. These things may not seem very big, but to the person who receives your kindness and mercy, you'll be a hero!

THOUGHT OF THE DAY

What are some ways you can be kind and merciful today?

PRAY TODAY

Dear God, please help me show Your kindness and mercy to everyone I meet. Amen.

HOW WILL THEY KNOW?

"This is how everyone will recognize that you are my disciples—when they see the love you have for each other."

JOHN 13:35 MSG

God wants everyone to know you love Him. And do you know the best way to show that you love God? Love people!

Jesus says followers of God should be great at loving others. But not just when it's easy! Anyone can do that. Jesus wants you to love all the time. So ask for God's help. Look for ways to be kind and care for all people, no matter what they say or do. When you do that, everyone will see what God's love really looks like!

THOUGHT OF THE DAY

Can you think of someone who is hard to love? How can you love him or her today?

PRAY TODAY

Dear God, I want people to know how much I love You! Please help me show love to everyone I meet today. Amen.

PRAY FOR EVERYBODY

Hatred stirs up trouble, but love forgives all wrongs.

PROVERBS 10:12 NCV

If someone has hurt you, what should you do? God says you should pray for them! Why is that?

Sitting around feeling angry or annoyed only makes you feel more angry and annoyed. Nothing gets better! But saying a prayer for that person can help. That's because prayer is a loving action. So you have to put unhappy feelings aside—at least for a little while—when you pray.

Ask God to bless the person you're upset with and to forgive them for hurting you. Your prayer might be exactly what that person needs! And you'll feel better too.

THOUGHT OF THE DAY

Prayer changes things, starting with your own heart!

PRAY TODAY

Dear God, it can be hard to pray for people who have hurt me. Please give me a loving heart. Amen.

A PROMISE YOU CAN SEE

"The rainbow that I have put in the sky will be my sign to you and to every living creature on earth."

GENESIS 9:12 CEV

God makes some important promises in the Bible. But one promise came with a picture: a rainbow!

God told Noah to build a giant boat (an "ark") and fill it with animals. Then God sent a huge flood to cover the whole world. But because Noah and his family obeyed God, they stayed safe. Afterward, God painted a rainbow in the sky as a promise. He promised never to flood the world again—and He never has!

You can't see every promise God makes. But every time you see a rainbow, you can remember that God's promises are real, and they're all around you!

THOUGHT OF THE DAY

Larry's favorite promise is that God will always be around! What's your favorite promise?

PRAY TODAY

Dear God, thank You for Your wonderful promises to me! Amen.

A SAFE PLACE

You are my hiding place and my shield; I hope in your word.

PSALM 119:114 NCV

God wants to give you courage and strength to do great things! But did you know He can also be a hiding place?

When you feel afraid or overwhelmed, you can go to God in prayer and rest with Him. Sometimes it helps to imagine climbing onto His lap or snuggling next to Him in a big comfy chair. You can also think about other ways the Bible describes God—as a shelter in a rainstorm or a sturdy place to stand when everything else is shaky. God is always with you. He is your special, safe hiding place.

THOUGHT OF THE DAY

It's impossible to hide from God, but you can always hide in God.

PRAY TODAY

Dear God, thank You for welcoming me into Your arms. Help me find rest in You. Amen.

READY TO RESIST

"Stay awake and pray for strength against temptation. The spirit wants to do what is right, but the body is weak."

MATTHEW 26:41 NCV

Everyone faces temptation now and then. Sometimes it's so hard to say no, even if you know something is wrong. What should you do when a friend starts to gossip or someone you admire asks you to break the rules?

Temptation can sneak up on you, so it's smart to have a plan. Talk to your parents about ways to stay strong when you feel tempted. Read your Bible, and learn how God helped others make good choices. Stay close to God, and you'll always be ready to resist!

THOUGHT OF THE DAY

Jesus used Bible verses to help Him fight temptation. Joseph simply ran away! What can you do?

PRAY TODAY

Dear God, You know what I need to say no to. Please give me strength and courage when I feel tempted! Amen.

RESPECT EVERYONE

Show respect for all people. Love the brothers and sisters of God's family.

1 PETER 2:17 ICB

I t's important to respect people who are in charge, like your parents and your teachers. But God wants us to treat *everyone* with respect. Respecting people means to treat them like they matter. And people matter to God.

Jesus showed respect to everyone He met, rich or poor. He respected His disciples by answering their questions and spending time with them. He even respected people nobody else liked because He knew that God loves everyone. When you show respect to others, you're acting like Jesus!

THOUGHT OF THE DAY

How can you show respect to the people you'll meet today?

PRAY TODAY

Dear God, You love everyone! Please help me to show respect to everyone around me. Amen.

THINK BEFORE YOU SPEAK

A kind answer soothes angry feelings, but harsh words stir them up.

PROVERBS 15:1 CEV

Words are very powerful! They can encourage, or they can hurt feelings. So you have to be careful when you use them.

When you're angry, it's especially easy to say things you might feel bad about later. So take a deep breath and think carefully before you say anything. Try replacing any angry words with kind words instead. That will keep you from hurting anyone's feelings, and it could also help solve the problem. Wise King Solomon tells us that angry words only make an argument worse. So be part of the solution instead!

THOUGHT OF THE DAY

Practice kind responses so you can be ready for any conversation.

PRAY TODAY

Dear God, it's hard to think when I get angry. Help me pause and think before I speak. Amen.

A GOOD EXAMPLE

"I have given you an example to follow. Do as I have done to you."

JOHN 13:15 NLT

Do you ever wonder how you should act? Just look at Jesus! In the Bible, Jesus says we can follow His example and treat people like He does. When you do that, *you* become an example too. Isn't that exciting?

But remember that none of us is perfect. So don't worry when you make mistakes! You can still be an example when you say sorry, fix what's wrong, and ask for forgiveness. Jesus wants us to follow His ways, share His love, and help where we can. When you are kind to everyone—including yourself!—you are doing exactly what He asked!

THOUGHT OF THE DAY

What's your favorite story about Jesus?

PRAY TODAY

Dear God, thank You for sending Jesus to be a perfect example for me to follow! Amen.

UNLIMITED FORGIVENESS

Then Peter came to him and asked, "Lord, how often should I forgive someone who sins against me? Seven times?" "No, not seven times," Jesus replied, "but seventy times seven!"

MATTHEW 18:21–22 NLT

Have you ever heard of a "second chance"? It means someone will let you try one more time to get things right. Well, God's forgiveness is all about giving you never-ending chances! Isn't that great?

God wants us to forgive that way too. It can be frustrating when someone keeps making mistakes, saying mean things, or irritating you. Don't give up on them! And don't bother keeping track. God will help you forgive again and again. Chances are, you'll love living a life of unlimited forgiveness!

THOUGHT OF THE DAY

God never gets tired of forgiving—and neither should we!

PRAY TODAY

Dear God, sometimes it's hard to forgive others. Please help me forgive again and again, just like You do. Amen.

KEEP ON ASKING

When doubts filled my mind, your comfort gave me renewed hope and cheer.

PSALM 94:19 NLT

You probably have lots of questions about God. That's no problem! He has all the answers you need.

Asking questions about God is called *seeking*. God wants us to seek Him, so don't ever be afraid to ask about things you don't understand. Talk to your parents or your Sunday school teacher. Be sure to read the Bible and ask God to make things clearer to you. The better you know God, the more comfort and joy you'll find in Him. So just keep on asking!

THOUGHT OF THE DAY

Jesus says that seeking leads to finding. So never stop seeking God!

PRAY TODAY

Dear God, please help me ask questions anytime I feel uncertain. Thank You for listening and answering! Amen.

A KIND WORD

How wonderful it is to be able to say the right thing at the right time!

PROVERBS 15:23 TLB

Saying kind words is one of the best ways to show God's love. And it's so easy! All you have to do is pay attention.

As you go through your day, look for people who need to hear something kind. Is someone left out on the playground? Does a friend feel sad today? Would your mom or dad like to hear you say that you appreciate the dinner they made? If you keep asking, God will show you people who need your kindness. And when you obey His guidance, you will make lots of people happy!

THOUGHT OF THE DAY

A kind word is always welcome.

PRAY TODAY

Dear God, please help me share kind words today. I want to make people happy! Amen.

SHARE GOD'S LOVE

"If you have two shirts, share with the person who does not have one. If you have food, share that too."

LUKE 3:11 ICB

What can you share with others? Clothes you don't wear much? Toys you don't play with? Sharing with others feels great. Even better, it's what God wants us to do!

God asks us to take care of each other by sharing what we have. You may not think you have much to give, but even small gifts can make a big difference. The Bible tells a story of a little boy who gave his small lunch to Jesus. Jesus used it to feed 5,000 people!

Ask God to show you how to share the things you have. He could help you change someone's life!

THOUGHT OF THE DAY

When you share with others, you share more than just things—you share God's love!

PRAY TODAY

Dear God, thank You for everything You've given me. Please help me share what I have with others. Amen.

GOD WILL MAKE THINGS RIGHT

God is fair and just; he corrects the misdirected, sends them in the right direction.

PSALM 25:8 MSG

God can always help you make things right. So when you make a mistake, don't worry! Just go to God. He will help you do whatever needs to be done. If you need to apologize to someone, He can give you the right words to say. If you need to fix something, He can give you strength and encouragement.

Making a poor choice is like turning the wrong way down a path. But God can turn you around so you're going the right direction again! All you have to do is ask.

THOUGHT OF THE DAY

God is ready and waiting to help, anytime you need Him!

PRAY TODAY

Dear God, I don't always make the best choices. Thank You that You love me and can help me make things right. Amen.

GOD'S PROMISE

"I assure you: Anyone who believes has eternal life."

JOHN 6:47 HCSB

God has made a great big promise: He will never leave you. In fact, He sent us His Son, Jesus, so that no one would ever have to be apart from Him. When you believe in Jesus, God lives in your heart every single day. And you get to live in heaven with Him forever!

Nothing will ever come between you and God. You can't lose Him, and He doesn't take breaks. Wherever you go, He is with you. No matter how many mistakes you make, He won't give up on you. His love is forever. That's a promise!

THOUGHT OF THE DAY

The gift of God's promise is free for everyone! All you have to do is say yes.

PRAY TODAY

Dear God, thank You for sending Jesus so we can always be together. I'm glad Your love is forever! Amen.

HEAVENLY PEACE

"I leave you peace. My peace I give you. I do not give it to you as the world does. So don't let your hearts be troubled."

JOHN 14:27 ICB

The Bible says that Jesus gives us peace. But His peace is very special. People can sometimes feel peaceful without Jesus, but only when everything goes their way. As soon as trouble comes, that kind of peace goes away. Then anger and fear take its place! But Jesus is stronger than that. He can keep your heart calm and joyful no matter what. Doesn't that sound great?

The best part about the peace of Jesus is that it's free! All you have to do is ask for it. With His perfect peace, you can face anything.

THOUGHT OF THE DAY
Jesus is sometimes called the Prince of Peace!

PRAY TODAY
Dear Jesus, You are all I need! Please come live in my heart so I can know Your peace. Amen.

STAY CALM

"The LORD himself will fight for you. Just stay calm."

EXODUS 14:14 NLT

The Israelites were so happy when Moses led them out of Egypt! But when they got to the Red Sea, they started to panic. Pharaoh's army was chasing them, and now they were trapped! But Moses told them to calm down and trust God. God had promised to save them, and God always keeps His promises.

When everything is going your way, faith in God is easy. But when things get hard, don't panic! God is still with you. Keep praying, and find comfort in His promise to give you all you need. Remember His goodness. Strong faith can help you stay calm no matter what happens!

THOUGHT OF THE DAY

Keep your faith strong by reading Bible stories and talking to God!

PRAY TODAY

Dear God, please strengthen my faith so I can stay calm and trust You, no matter what happens. Amen.

GOD GUIDES YOUR STEPS

A man's heart plans his way, but the LORD determines his steps.

PROVERBS 16:9 HCSB

What do you want to be when you grow up? It's so much fun to dream about the future! And now is the perfect time to learn all you can about the things you love to do.

God wants you to work hard for your dreams. But He also wants you to stay close to Him and listen to His direction. We can make plans, but the Bible says God directs our steps. So be sure to keep praying and listening to God. He will tell you which way to go so you end up where He knows you should be!

THOUGHT OF THE DAY
Your future is in good hands—God's!

PRAY TODAY
Dear God, I'm so excited to become who You want me to be! Help me listen to Your direction and work hard. Amen.

HARD CHANGES

There is a time for everything, and a season for every activity under the heavens.

ECCLESIASTES 3:1 NIV

Some changes are easy. You can probably change your pajamas with no problem! But some changes—even good ones—can be hard. Moving to a new town or starting a different grade in school or welcoming a new sibling are all big changes that can bring lots of feelings. You might feel happy, sad, excited, mad, and nervous all at the same time. That's perfectly OK! Talk to your parents about it. Ask about a time they went through a big change. And remember to pray too. God can use changes to help you grow, learn, and find joy!

THOUGHT OF THE DAY

One thing NEVER changes: God's love!

PRAY TODAY

Dear God, sometimes I don't want things to change. Help me remember Your love and find joy in each new thing! Amen.

GOD'S ALWAYS THERE

"Do not be afraid or discouraged. For the LORD your God is with you wherever you go."

JOSHUA 1:9 NLT

When you have a great day, it's easy to remember God! You might even feel extra close to Him. But when you have a bad day, guess what? God is still right beside you.

We all go through hard times. And it's normal to feel lonely during those times. But you are never truly alone because God will never leave you. And you can talk with Him about anything! He loves to comfort you. So next time you feel upset or lonely, imagine God giving you a big hug. He's always around!

THOUGHT OF THE DAY

God's beside you every day. Nothing makes Him go away.

PRAY TODAY

Dear God, I'm so glad You will never leave me. Help me remember to talk to You when I'm feeling down. Amen.

GENTLE AND CALM

Always be gentle with others. The Lord will soon be here.

PHILIPPIANS 4:5 CEV

God says to be gentle with each other. What does that mean?

We're gentle when we act calmly. It can be hard to control our bodies and words sometimes. But when you speak or behave roughly, you might hurt someone! You could hurt their bodies by hitting or pushing. You could hurt their feelings by yelling or breaking something that belongs to them. Remember that everyone is part of God's family—even people who make you mad. And God doesn't want any of His children to get hurt. So ask Him to help you choose gentleness all the time!

THOUGHT OF THE DAY

When you feel out of control, try taking a deep breath before you do anything. It will give you time to choose a gentle action!

PRAY TODAY

Dear God, sometimes it's SO HARD to be gentle. Help me calm down so I can treat everyone gently every day. Amen.

CHEERFUL WORKERS

Work hard and cheerfully at all you do, just as though you were working for the Lord.

COLOSSIANS 3:23 TLB

D o you know that God cares about *how* you work? In the Bible, He says to work hard, but also to be a cheerful worker!

Your chores or schoolwork may not always seem like fun, but have you ever thought about making up games when you do them? Maybe you can time yourself and see if you can finish faster than last time. Or maybe you can make up a song or a story as you do your chores. Working cheerfully at everything you do is the best way to get the job done!

THOUGHT OF THE DAY

What is one way to make your work more cheerful today?

PRAY TODAY

Dear God, thanks for giving me work to do. Please help me to be a cheerful worker. Amen.

PARTY TIME!

So rejoice in the LORD and be glad, all you who obey him!
Shout for joy, all you whose hearts are pure!

PSALM 32:11 NLT

Can you think of a time you went to a party? Maybe you had a birthday party, or you celebrated a big holiday with your family. Isn't it fun to be happy and joyful together?

Guess what? You could have a party every day just by praising God! He is so good, and He loves us very much. He gave us the Bible so we could get to know Him and learn how to live a great life. He even sent Jesus so we can live with Him forever. Those are all reasons to celebrate! So sing, dance, and tell your friends. It's a God party!

THOUGHT OF THE DAY

If you threw a God party, what would it look like?

PRAY TODAY

Dear God, hooray for You! I am so glad to be Your child, and I want to celebrate You every day! Amen.

BETTER TOGETHER

Two can accomplish more than twice as much as one, for the results can be much better. If one falls, the other pulls him up; but if a man falls when he is alone, he's in trouble.

ECCLESIASTES 4:9-10 TLB

What do you like to do with your friends? Play pretend? Build things? Make up new games? Friends make everything better! And not because they always do what we say or let us have our own way. Friends have the most fun when we listen to each other's ideas and create something together!

God says that when people are true friends, they can do amazing things. By working together, we can build and solve and imagine things that no one could do all alone. And if we make mistakes, our friends help us make things right again. True friends are gifts from God!

THOUGHT OF THE DAY

Who is one of your true friends? Thank God for him or her today!

PRAY TODAY

Dear God, thank You for friendship! Please help me to be a true friend today and every day. Amen.

FAMILY RESEMBLANCE

So God created human beings in his own image.

GENESIS 1:27A NLT

Sometimes kids look like their parents. Maybe your hair is curly like your mom's, or your eyes are the same color as your dad's. That's called family resemblance. And it happens in God's family too!

The Bible says God made people in His image—so we all look a little like Him! Just like God, we can feel and share love, enjoy beautiful things, and make good choices. And when we treat people kindly and choose to help instead of hurt, others will see God in us! What a great family resemblance!

THOUGHT OF THE DAY

How can you show someone what God looks like today?

PRAY TODAY

Dear God, thank You for creating me to be Your child! I love being in Your family. Amen.

IT'S ALL FORGOTTEN

You will throw away all our sins into the deepest part of the sea.

MICAH 7:19B NCV

If you want to know what true forgiveness looks like, just watch how God does it. He doesn't secretly stay mad while pretending everything is OK. He doesn't remind us of our mistakes all the time. Instead, when we tell God we're sorry, He just forgives us—right away and all the way! In fact, the Bible says it's like God throws our sins to the bottom of the ocean where no one can reach them. He doesn't pay attention to them anymore! We get a fresh new start with God anytime we ask. Isn't that wonderful news?

THOUGHT OF THE DAY

God's forgiveness is forever!

PRAY TODAY

Dear God, thank You for forgiving me no matter what! Help me to forgive others just like You: right away and all the way! Amen.

JUST TALK TO GOD

I prayed to the Lord, and he answered me. He freed me from all my fears.

PSALM 34:4 NLT

It's normal to feel frightened sometimes. Even brave King David felt afraid! But talking to God helped him feel better.

You can talk to God too. God loves to hear what you're thinking about! Try telling God about what scares you, and ask Him to take away your fear. Remember that God loves you. He is more powerful than anything, and He wants to help you feel happy and safe. All you have to do is ask Him!

THOUGHT OF THE DAY

God will always hear your prayer.

PRAY TODAY

Dear Lord, thank You for being with me all the time, even when I feel afraid. Amen.

JUST THE WAY YOU ARE

"You're blessed when you're content with just who you are—no more, no less."

MATTHEW 5:5 MSG

God wants us to do our best. That means working hard at school, being kind to others, and practicing the gifts and talents He gives us. But it doesn't mean we have to be perfect.

No one is perfect! Everyone makes mistakes, and everyone needs God's help. So be kind to yourself. Try new things, and remember that you're allowed to mess up. After all, mistakes help you learn! Don't compare yourself to anyone else. Everyone has unique gifts and abilities. You are exactly who God wants you to be.

THOUGHT OF THE DAY

What is something you are good at? What's something you'd like to try?

PRAY TODAY

Dear God, thank You for loving me just the way I am! Amen.

WHOM WILL YOU CHOOSE?

"Choose this day whom you will serve. . . . But as for me and my house, we will serve the LORD."

JOSHUA 24:15 ESV

The Bible tells us about a man named Joshua, who had to decide whether to serve God or himself. He chose to serve God, and God was pleased.

You get to make the same kind of choice that Joshua did. Serving God means doing what God wants you to do. You can serve God by being kind to others, obeying your parents, and sharing what you have.

Joshua knew that God loved him and wanted what was best for him. That is why he chose to serve God. God also loves you and wants what is best for you. Whom will you choose to serve?

THOUGHT OF THE DAY

Choosing to serve God is always the best choice!

PRAY TODAY

Dear God, thank You for choosing to love me. Please help me choose to serve You. Amen.

TRUTH TOOLS

Stand firm then, with the belt of truth buckled around your waist.

EPHESIANS 6:14A NIV

Do you ever feel like disobeying God? Or maybe He sometimes seems far away? The Bible says God gives us something special to help us stay strong: the Belt of Truth!

Think of the Belt of Truth like a cool tool belt that you can pack full of truths about God. Truth Tool #1: God loves you! Truth Tool #2: God wants you to treat others kindly. Fill your tool belt by learning Bible verses, listening to Bible stories, and talking with God. Then no matter what happens, you'll always be ready to whip out a Truth Tool!

THOUGHT OF THE DAY

What Truth Tool can you find in your favorite Bible story?

PRAY TODAY

Dear God, please help me learn Your truths so I can do the right thing and follow You no matter what! Amen.

GOD KNOWS BEST

*"Be strong and courageous. Do not be afraid or terrified because of them, for the L*ORD *your God goes with you; he will never leave you nor forsake you."*

DEUTERONOMY 31:6 NIV

Gideon was a soldier who wanted to do well and please God. But one day, God told him to lead a tiny army against an enemy that had a huge army! Gideon felt scared, but God promised to help him. So Gideon did exactly what God said, and his army won the battle!

God might not ask you to lead an army. But maybe you need to do something else that takes courage—like moving to a new school or saying no when a friend wants you to break the rules. Ask God to help you feel brave. With Him, you can do anything!

THOUGHT OF THE DAY

Be brave and follow God. He's got the best ideas!

PRAY TODAY

Dear God, I want to be brave like Gideon. Please give me courage to do whatever You have in mind for me! Amen.

STAY STRONG WITH GOD

"Be strong! Be courageous! Do not be afraid of them! For the Lord your God will be with you. He will neither fail you nor forsake you."

DEUTERONOMY 31:6 TLB

It's hard to do the right thing when other people do not want you to. Daniel was a young man in Bible times who wasn't afraid to do the right thing. The people around him wanted him to stop praying to God. But Daniel would not stop praying. So the people put Daniel into a den of hungry lions to punish him, but Daniel still kept praying. Then do you know what happened? God shut the lions' mouths and protected Daniel!

God says that you can be strong and filled with courage too. You can always trust God to help you do the right thing.

THOUGHT OF THE DAY

If you keep from doing wrong, God says He will keep you strong!

PRAY TODAY

Dear God, I want to be strong and courageous. Help me do the right thing, even if it's hard. Amen.

LET'S GET ALONG

Work at getting along with each other and with God.

HEBREWS 12:14 MSG

D o you get along with God? If you try to follow what He says, then you probably do! Getting along with God means you spend time reading the Bible and praying, and you work hard to follow His ways.

God also wants us to get along with other people. You won't always agree with everyone, but that's OK. When you listen to others, share God's love, and help people in need, you are doing what God asks. And when you get along with others and with God, you help everyone see that God is good and loving.

THOUGHT OF THE DAY

When you get along with God, He'll help you get along with others!

PRAY TODAY

Dear God, please help me do what You want me to do. I want everyone to know how much You love us. Amen.

SHARING IS BETTER

And God will generously provide all you need. Then you will always have everything you need and plenty left over to share with others.

2 CORINTHIANS 9:8 NLT

God has promised to give you everything you need. It's a blessing to be taken care of so well.

Sometimes we forget that God is taking care of us, and we start feeling unhappy about things we don't have. We think that getting more stuff will make us happy. God wants us to trust Him and trust that He will choose to provide in just the right way. And He wants to build a generous heart in each of us so that we will want to share with others. Giving makes your heart happier!

THOUGHT OF THE DAY

Is there something you can share with someone else today?

PRAY TODAY

Dear God, thank You for taking care of me! Help me to have a generous heart. Amen.

GROWING IN GOD

. . . so that you will live the kind of life that honors and pleases the Lord in every way. You will produce fruit in every good work and grow in the knowledge of God.

COLOSSIANS 1:10 NCV

Life with God is an amazing adventure. There's always something new to discover!

Even your Sunday school teachers and your pastors are still learning about God. That's because He does new things every day. He shows us new ways to love each other and to love Him. Sometimes you'll think you totally understand something in the Bible, and then He'll show you a brand-new way to think about it! So never stop following God, asking questions, and learning about His wonderful ways. You never know what you might find!

THOUGHT OF THE DAY

God can help you learn and grow. There's always something new to know!

PRAY TODAY

Dear God, I love being on this adventure with You! Help my knowledge of You grow a little more each day. Amen.

HONESTY AND KINDNESS

In every way be an example of doing good deeds. When you teach, do it with honesty and seriousness.

TITUS 2:7 NCV

God wants us to be honest and kind. When honesty and kindness work together, it makes you a friend that people know they can depend on.

When we tell the truth, God wants to help us do that with love. It may take practice, but God can help! Ask God to show you how to be honest and kind today.

THOUGHT OF THE DAY

It's good to be both honest and kind at the same time, as much as possible. Be looking for ways to do that today.

PRAY TODAY

Dear God, please help me to be truthful and kind so I can show Your love to others. Amen.

WHAT A BLESSING

"But blessed are those who trust in the Lord and have made the Lord their hope and confidence."

JEREMIAH 17:7 NLT

Today's Bible verse says if we believe and trust in God, we are blessed. But what does it mean to be blessed? Believing and trusting in God makes us feel safe and peaceful. That's being blessed. Knowing how much God loves us and sharing His love with others gives us joy. That's being blessed. Understanding that God has a wonderful plan for our lives gives us peace. That's being blessed. No matter what happens around us, when we know that God is with us, we don't need to worry. We are blessed!

THOUGHT OF THE DAY

What are some ways God has blessed you?

PRAY TODAY

Dear God, thank You for always being with me, loving me, and blessing me. Amen.

HAPPY INSIDE OUT

I'm happy from the inside out, and from the outside in, I'm firmly formed.

PSALM 16:9 MSG

How do you tell if someone is happy? Since we can't see feelings, we usually look at the outside to see how someone feels on the inside. If someone is stomping around with a frown on her face, we can be pretty sure that she's mad or sad. But when a person is feeling happy, he'll usually smile or laugh or sing or dance or even try to make others happy. The Bible says it's good to show your happy feelings from the inside out! So share your happiness with someone else today!

THOUGHT OF THE DAY

Turn your frown upside down, and share a smile today!

PRAY TODAY

Dear God, thank You for giving me so much to be happy about. Please help me to share my happiness from the inside out! Amen.

HE HEARS YOU

"Then if my people who are called by my name will humble themselves and pray and seek my face and turn from their wicked ways, I will hear from heaven and will forgive their sins and restore their land."

2 CHRONICLES 7:14 NLT

God says He wants His people to be humble. That means He wants us to ask Him for help when we don't know what to do. He promises to hear us, forgive us, and help us.

Being humble also means trusting that God's ways are the best ways. He can help you through anything. Even if you have done something wrong, don't be afraid to tell God what is in your heart. He always listens, and He always loves you.

THOUGHT OF THE DAY

Take time every day to ask God what He wants you to do.

PRAY TODAY

Dear God, I know You will never leave me. Thank You for hearing my prayers and for always loving me. Amen.

TALKING TO GOD

I cried to him for help; I praised him with songs.

PSALM 66:17 GNT

God is always ready to hear from you. He loves for you to tell Him all about what you're feeling! And do you know that God loves to talk to you too?

You can't hear God like you can hear another person's voice, but He's still telling you things. He might bring a new friend into your life or show you someone who needs your help. He might help you feel better when you're sad. But the best way to hear God is through the Bible. The more you learn about the Bible, the more you'll recognize God's special voice. Pretty soon, you'll hear Him everywhere!

THOUGHT OF THE DAY

Practice talking and listening to God every day. You never know what He'll say next!

PRAY TODAY

Dear God, thank You that You want to hear from me! Please help me listen for Your voice too. Amen.

THE GIFT OF PEACE

"Peace I leave with you; my peace I give you. I do not give to you as the world gives. Do not let your hearts be troubled and do not be afraid."

JOHN 14:27 NIV

Do you know what it means to be peaceful? People are "at peace" when they are not afraid. That doesn't mean everything is easy for them. It just means they trust God to take care of them!

Jesus knows it's sometimes hard to feel peaceful. That's why He offers us *His* peace. His peace is perfect, and He has plenty to share. Next time you feel scared, ask Jesus to give you His gift of peace. He is always with you! He wants to comfort you and give you everything you need.

THOUGHT OF THE DAY

Why do you think God wants you to feel peaceful?

PRAY TODAY

Dear God, thank You for the gift of peace. Help me trust You more each day. Amen.

GOD'S CRAZY PLANS

"Do you think you can explain the mystery of God? Do you think you can diagram God Almighty? God is far higher than you can imagine, far deeper than you can comprehend."

JOB 11:7-8 MSG

God asked people to do some pretty weird things in the Bible. He told Noah to build a huge boat in the middle of the desert! All of Noah's friends must have thought he was crazy, but Noah trusted God. When he finally finished the boat, the rain fell hard, and water covered the earth. Now that boat made sense! You won't know why God does everything He does. Sometimes it might look like nothing makes sense. But remember Noah and the flood. God has a plan for everything. Trust Him completely and watch what happens!

THOUGHT OF THE DAY

God knows what He's doing, so you don't need to worry.

PRAY TODAY

Dear God, help me trust Your plan, even when it doesn't make sense to me! Amen.

BE BRAVE!

"Don't worry about this Philistine," David told Saul. "I'll go fight him!"

1 SAMUEL 17:32 NLT

The next time you're reading your Bible, check out the story of David and Goliath. Goliath was a big, strong soldier who was saying bad things about God's people. Everyone was afraid to fight him, but David knew what Goliath was doing was wrong. So even though David wasn't a soldier, he used whatever God gave him to stand up for what was right.

God helped David to be brave so he could face Goliath. He can make you brave too! If you see something happening that seems wrong, ask God for the courage to fix it. God can help you do anything!

THOUGHT OF THE DAY

Trust God, and He will help you be brave!

PRAY TODAY

Dear God, please give me courage to do hard things. I can do anything by Your side. Amen.

FRIENDS WHO MAKE YOU BETTER

As iron sharpens iron, so people can improve each other.

PROVERBS 27:17 NCV

What are some things you like about your friends? The Bible says that great friends help each other be the very best they can be. They encourage each other to do good and work hard. God wants you to find those kinds of friends. They build you up and help you grow!

If a friend ever pushes you to do something wrong, he or she isn't a very good friend. Be firm, and say no. Then look for friends who are kind and will help you make good decisions. You'll be glad you did!

THOUGHT OF THE DAY

Who is one of your good friends? What do you like to do together?

PRAY TODAY

Dear God, please help me make friends who are kind and encouraging. And help me to be that kind of friend too! Amen.

BUILDING A STRONG FAITH

Those with pure hearts shall become stronger and stronger.

JOB 17:9 TLB

When you run and jump and climb, your muscles get stronger. Do you know you can make your faith strong too? The Bible says that when we have pure hearts, our faith gets stronger! What can we do to make our hearts pure?

Start by reading Bible stories and memorizing verses from God's Word. Then practice what you learn: show kindness to others, help people who are hurting, and pray for people in need. These are the kinds of things Jesus did. As you follow Him, your heart becomes purer and your faith grows stronger and stronger!

THOUGHT OF THE DAY

What are some faith exercises you can do today?

PRAY TODAY

Dear God, please help me keep my heart pure so I can have a strong and growing faith. Amen.

FINDING WISDOM

For wisdom is far more valuable than rubies. Nothing you desire can compare with it.

PROVERBS 8:11 NLT

The Bible tells us about a king named Solomon. He had a chance to ask God for anything in the world! But he didn't ask for money or power. Solomon asked for wisdom. He knew that the most important thing he could do was make wise choices.

Do you know that you can be like King Solomon? Whenever you aren't sure what to do, just ask God to help you. He promises to give you wisdom too! As long as you ask God for wisdom and do your best to follow what He says, you can count on making great choices!

THOUGHT OF THE DAY

Can you think of a time you made a wise choice?

PRAY TODAY

Dear God, I want to be wise and make good choices. Please help me remember to ask You for help every day. Amen.

HOPE-FULL

I pray that the God who gives hope will fill you with much joy and peace while you trust in him. Then your hope will overflow by the power of the Holy Spirit.

ROMANS 15:13 ICB

Have you ever been so happy you couldn't wait to share it with someone? That's what God's hope is like!

Hope comes from believing that God will always help you. Even if things don't go the way you'd like, you can have hope that God will lead you to new things He's planned just for you. That's pretty exciting! God's hope can fill you with so much joy that you'll want to share it with others. So go for it! You never know who might need to hear about God's hope.

THOUGHT OF THE DAY

When your joy overflows, share it with others!

PRAY TODAY

Dear God, I am so glad You always help me! Please show me how I can share Your hope with others. Amen.

HOW WOULD YOU FEEL?

For if you refuse to act kindly, you can hardly expect to be treated kindly. Kind mercy wins over harsh judgment every time.

JAMES 2:12–13 MSG

Has someone ever been mean to you? It feels pretty bad! Wouldn't you rather be treated kindly? Guess what? So would everyone else!

God wants us to have empathy—that means we should think about how our actions and words make other people feel. If it's hard to imagine someone else's feelings, ask yourself how YOU would feel. Then choose words that you would like to hear. When you are thoughtful about what you say and do, your kindness will probably be returned!

THOUGHT OF THE DAY

When in doubt, choose kindness over meanness every time.

PRAY TODAY

Dear God, please help me always to think before I speak. I like being treated with kindness, and I know others do too! Amen.

PERFECT TIMING

But they that wait upon the Lord shall renew their strength;
they shall mount up with wings as eagles; they shall run,
and not be weary; and they shall walk, and not faint.

ISAIAH 40:31 KJV

God knows what you need and when you need it. He loves you! And He promises to help you learn and grow so you can do the great things He's planned for you.

Sometimes it can feel like God moves really slowly. Maybe you're impatient to know what God has in store for you. Or you have big dreams that you want to do RIGHT NOW! But the Bible says that when we wait for God to help us, we'll be able to do much more than we can even imagine. That's exciting! So trust God. His timing is perfect!

THOUGHT OF THE DAY

God's timing isn't the same as our timing—it's better!

PRAY TODAY

Dear God, thank You for making big plans for me! Help me to be patient and trust Your timing. Amen.

STAYING SAFE

A person without self-control is like a city with broken-down walls.

PROVERBS 25:28 NLT

The Bible says that having self-control keeps you safe, but losing self-control is dangerous. Do you know why?

When we lose self-control, we sometimes say unkind words or even do things that hurt another person. Being self-controlled might mean waiting for something that you want right now or taking turns instead of always being first. Self-control helps you say words that help instead of words that hurt. It isn't always the easy way, but it is always the best way.

THOUGHT OF THE DAY

When is it hard for you to practice self-control?

PRAY TODAY

Dear God, thank You for helping me get better at self-control so I can be safe and happy. Amen.

ALWAYS DO WHAT'S RIGHT

So let's not allow ourselves to get fatigued doing good. At the right time we will harvest a good crop if we don't give up, or quit.

GALATIANS 6:9 MSG

Making right choices is always good, but sometimes it is hard to do. Maybe your friends are making a poor choice and they want you to do the same thing. What will you do then?

It helps to remember that God loves you and is watching over you. He wants to help you do what is right, even when it's hard. Ask Him to give you courage to make good choices. He promises to surprise you with blessings when you follow Him!

THOUGHT OF THE DAY

When you need to make a choice about doing what is right, always ask God for His help.

PRAY TODAY

Dear God, I'm so glad You love me and want me to do what is right. Help me remember to call on You when I have to make hard choices. Amen.

YOU CAN DO ANYTHING!

Jesus replied, "Why do you say 'if you can'? Anything is possible for someone who has faith!"

MARK 9:23 CEV

What is something big you want to do? It's exciting to have dreams and goals! God tells us to dream big, work hard, and have faith in Him. He has great plans for you, and He can help you accomplish anything.

Sometimes that's hard to remember. Maybe learning a new skill takes longer than you thought it would, or somebody says something discouraging. Don't give up! Go back to God and remember His promises. Have faith that He loves you and cares about your dreams. Trust that He will never leave you. With God by your side, nothing is impossible!

THOUGHT OF THE DAY

Your big dreams are gifts from God. He gave them to you for a reason!

PRAY TODAY

Dear God, thank You for caring about the things I care about. Help me have strong faith in You as I dream big dreams! Amen.

JOYFUL LIVING

"You will live in joy and peace."

ISAIAH 55:12A NLT

o you start your day with a smile or a frown? Are your words kind or unkind? When someone asks you a question, do you listen, or do you ignore them? If you want to have a joyful life, you can choose to be a good listener, smile often, and say kind things to others. When you do these things, others want to be your friend, and you will find that your life is filled with joy and peace. Ask God to help you begin each day with joy. He'll do it! Then you will truly have a joyful life.

THOUGHT OF THE DAY

Start each day by following God's way to live with joy and peace.

PRAY TODAY

Dear God, please fill my heart with Your joy every day. Amen.

DOING LOVE

My children, our love should not be only words and talk. Our love must be true love. And we should show that love by what we do.

1 John 3:18 icb

Many people think that love is a feeling. But the Bible says that love is something we do. If we say we love someone, but we don't act in loving ways, then we are not telling the truth. If a friend is sad, you can show your love by listening to him or her and spending time together. If your parents ask you to help at home, you can show them your love by helping without complaining. It is good to tell others that we love them, but the Bible says that *doing* love is even better!

THOUGHT OF THE DAY

Try to think of three different ways to "do love" today.

PRAY TODAY

Dear God, thank You for loving me. Help me show my love to others by doing kind, patient, and caring things for them. Amen.

HAPPY THOUGHTS

Those who are pure in their thinking are happy. They will be with God.

MATTHEW 5:8 ICB

Have you ever noticed that if you think about a sad story or an exciting moment, you start to feel sad or excited all over again? That's because what you think about can actually change the way you feel!

God wants us to feel joyful, so He tells us not to dwell on thoughts that make us angry or upset. Instead, think about things that come from Him, like your family, fun times with your friends, and His amazing love. That way, you will be filled with God's joy!

THOUGHT OF THE DAY

Find a happy thought for today, and hang on to it no matter what!

PRAY TODAY

Dear God, please help me think about only good things today. I want to feel Your joy! Amen.

JUST BELIEVE!

"Don't be afraid; just believe."

MARK 5:36 NIV

Learning new things can be exciting! But sometimes it's hard to be brave enough to try something new. Well, God doesn't want you to miss out on anything because you're afraid. So He says all you need to do is believe in Him.

Believe He loves you enough to help you grow and get better. Believe He is strong enough to help you up when you fall. When you believe that God is by your side, things don't seem so scary. Then you can try anything!

THOUGHT OF THE DAY

Trust that God will help you through anything you want to do!

PRAY TODAY

Dear God, help me believe that You are always with me. Together we can do anything! Amen.

TURN YOUR FROWN UPSIDE DOWN!

A cheerful look brings joy to the heart; good news makes for good health.

PROVERBS 15:30 NLT

Have you ever noticed how being around a frowning person can make you feel sad too? But what happens when you are around a smiling person?

The Bible reminds us that we can share our happiness with others. And when we belong to Jesus, we have lots to smile about! We know that He loves us and will never leave us. We know that He hears our prayers. We know that every good thing we have comes from Him. When you think of all your blessings, it's easy to turn a frown up-side down into a smile. Try it! You'll feel better, and so will everyone around you!

THOUGHT OF THE DAY

Think about a time when someone's smile made you feel better.

PRAY TODAY

Dear God, when I'm feeling sad, please help me remember all the ways You show me You love me. Amen.

HOW TO KNOW GOD

This is how we are sure that we have come to know Him: by keeping His commands.

1 JOHN 2:3 HCSB

How can you really know God? Can you visit Him? Can you take him to Show and Tell? Can you invite Him to dinner? Not exactly! But the Bible says that we can know God by *doing* what He says.

We learn what God says by reading the Bible and going to church. Then we have to ACT! When we love one another, we love like God loves. When we tell the truth, we are doing what God does. We get closer to God when we act the way He tells us to. So if you want to know God, try following His commands!

THOUGHT OF THE DAY

Read your Bible and do what God says. That's the best way to know God better!

PRAY TODAY

Dear God, I want to know You better each day. Please help me do just what You say. Amen.

A REASON TO HOPE

May the God of hope fill you with all joy and peace as you trust in him, so that you may overflow with hope by the power of the Holy Spirit.

ROMANS 15:13 NIV

Hope means more than just wanting something. It means to expect things with confidence and trust. When you pray, be confident that God hears you. Expect Him to answer in the way He sees is best. When you need peace and comfort, trust that He will give them to you. God has promised to take care of each of us. And God always keeps His promises—just ask anyone in the Bible! So don't get discouraged. As a member of God's family, you always have a reason to hope.

THOUGHT OF THE DAY

Hope is a powerful thing—it can bring you peace and joy!

PRAY TODAY

Dear God, thank You that I can trust You with confidence. Please help me remember that when I feel discouraged. Amen.

YOU CAN ALWAYS TRUST GOD

Commit everything you do to the LORD. Trust him, and he will help you.

PSALM 37:5 NLT

You might not always understand what God is doing. But you can always trust that He is in control.

It's normal to want to be in charge of everything. Especially if you think your ideas are the best! But God wants us to remember that He's really in charge. So don't worry if things don't happen the way you expected. Try not to get upset if you don't get what you want right away. Pray for God's help, and trust Him to take care of you. He always will.

THOUGHT OF THE DAY

How does it feel to know that God is in control of everything?

PRAY TODAY

Dear God, help me remember that You control everything, not me! Thank You that I can trust You all the time. Amen.

FRIENDS HELP FRIENDS

You use steel to sharpen steel, and one friend sharpens another.

PROVERBS 27:17 MSG

There are many ways that friends help one another. One way you might not know about is how one friend can "sharpen" another.

The Bible verse above talks about using steel to sharpen steel. When two pieces of steel are rubbed together, they make each other sharp by smoothing out rough edges. Friends sharpen one another when they help the other person make good choices. Sometimes a friend needs to be reminded to be kinder or to try harder. That's not always easy to hear—or say!—but good friends listen and learn from one another. Then they each become better!

THOUGHT OF THE DAY

Friends who help each other grow are the best friends we can know!

PRAY TODAY

Dear God, thanks for giving me good friends who love me and help me grow. Help me to be a good friend too. Amen.

WONDERFULLY MADE

I will praise You because I have been remarkably and wonderfully made.

PSALM 139:14A HCSB

Have you ever looked at an invention and wondered who made it? How did they decide to put it together? How did they make it work just right? Well, *you* are one of the most amazing creations in the world. Do you know that you have been made by God? He decided just the right way to make you, and He says you are remarkable and wonderful! Even if there are times when you don't feel very special, God says you are! You can trust that God made you exactly the way you should be. He loves you and has great plans for you.

THOUGHT OF THE DAY

You are a wonderful creation, made by God.

PRAY TODAY

Thank You, God, for loving me and making me just the way You wanted me to be. Amen.

DO GREAT THINGS!

You are young, but do not let anyone treat you as if you were not important. Be an example to show the believers how they should live. Show them with your words, with the way you live, with your love, with your faith, and with your pure life.

1 TIMOTHY 4:12 ICB

When we trust God, He is always with us, and we can show His love to others no matter how old we are!

God can work through you today. Is there someone you know who needs a little help? Maybe a new neighbor would like to be friends or someone at church could use a hug. You could even ask your parents if you can give away clothes or books to kids who don't have enough. Your kind actions will show everyone that God loves us.

THOUGHT OF THE DAY

Do you have an idea that could help someone? Don't be afraid to try! Maybe your parents can help you make it happen.

PRAY TODAY

Dear God, thank You that I am important, even though I'm young. Help me do what I can to make a difference every day. Amen.

GOD'S VIP

Do not be lazy but work hard, serving the Lord with all your heart.

ROMANS 12:11 NCV

Someone who is rich and famous is sometimes called a VIP—a Very Important Person. But Jesus says that the most important people are those who serve others. That means anyone can be God's VIP!

Serving someone can look like all kinds of things. You could make a card for a sick neighbor or offer to take your friend's dog for a walk. Maybe a younger friend or sibling is learning something new. Can you help? Look for ways to help all the people in your life. God needs you to be His VIP!

THOUGHT OF THE DAY

When you work hard to serve someone else, God blesses both of you.

PRAY TODAY

Dear Jesus, I want to be Your VIP. Please show me how I can serve the people around me, and help me work hard! Amen.

THE BEST LOVE

This is what real love is: It is not our love for God; it is God's love for us. He sent his Son to . . . take away our sins.

1 JOHN 4:10 NCV

God sure loves you a lot. In fact, the Bible tells us if we want to know what real love looks like, all we have to do is look at how God loves us. God sent His Son, Jesus, to save us. Now, because of Jesus, anyone can choose to live with God forever. No one is perfect, and we all make mistakes, but that doesn't change God's love. He loves you the way you are, now and forever.

So give thanks for God's perfect love. It's the very best love there is. And it's yours!

THOUGHT OF THE DAY

God's love is free. You don't have to earn it, and you can never lose it.

PRAY TODAY

Dear God, I love You! Thank You for showing us what love means by sending Jesus to save us. Amen.

A STRONG VINE

"Yes, I am the Vine; you are the branches. Whoever lives in me and I in him shall produce a large crop of fruit. For apart from me you can't do a thing."

JOHN 15:5 TLB

Do you know how grapes grow? Clusters of grapes grow on strong vines that provide everything they need. One single vine can produce lots of big, juicy grapes!

Jesus tells us that we should think of Him like a strong vine. He gives us all we need to do amazing things! We don't have to look anywhere else for love or joy or strength—Jesus has it all. So stay connected to Jesus. He'll give you an abundant life, full of His blessings!

THOUGHT OF THE DAY

You can connect to Jesus by praying, reading your Bible, and going to church!

PRAY TODAY

Dear God, thank You for being the source of everything I need. I want to stay with You forever! Amen.

SHOW AND TELL

Here's what you do: Live well, live wisely, live humbly. It's the way you live, not the way you talk, that counts.

JAMES 3:13 MSG

It's good to say things like "Thank you," "I'm sorry," and "I love you." But God wants us to follow those words with actions. He wants us to show *and* tell!

How can you show your love for others? Maybe you can share a favorite toy with a friend. How can you show you are thankful? What about helping your mom or dad clean up after dinner? And any time you say "I'm sorry," you can work hard to make things right. God can help you speak and act in loving ways every day!

THOUGHT OF THE DAY

Be kind in everything you say. Then be sure to act that way!

PRAY TODAY

Dear God, help me show love to everyone with both my words and my actions. Amen.

A RELUCTANT HERO

"So be strong and courageous! Do not be afraid and do not panic before them. For the LORD your God will personally go ahead of you. He will neither fail you nor abandon you."

DEUTERONOMY 31:6 NLT

The Bible says to be strong and brave. But it tells the story of Gideon, who didn't think he was strong and brave at all. He thought he was too small and weak to do anything for God, but God knew better. He needed Gideon to lead the army so God could save His people from an enemy. After a while, Gideon finally said yes. He trusted God and obeyed Him, and God's army won the battle.

You can trust that God knows the right plans for you, so don't be afraid. Be strong and courageous—just like Gideon!

THOUGHT OF THE DAY

God will never set you up for failure. He wants you to succeed!

PRAY TODAY

Dear God, I don't know what You have planned for me, but help me to be ready and brave when it is time. Amen.

LOVE AND LOYALTY

But Ruth replied, "Don't ask me to leave you and turn back. Wherever you go, I will go; wherever you live, I will live. Your people will be my people, and your God will be my God."

RUTH 1:16 NLT

God puts people into families so we can learn how to live and love. Parents, children, grandparents, and cousins all share together during fun times and hard times. When someone in a family needs help, the whole family helps. When someone in a family is happy, the whole family celebrates. In families, we learn how to love each other and how to be there for one another. That is called loyalty. God asks us to be loyal to our families and to Him. It's one of the best ways to show your love!

THOUGHT OF THE DAY

How can you show loyalty to someone in your family today?

PRAY TODAY

Dear God, thank You for my family. Help me to always be loving and loyal to them and to You. Amen.

SHOWING RESPECT

Treat others just as you want to be treated.

LUKE 6:31 CEV

How do you feel when someone takes your things without asking? What if you give a friend a gift and he or she doesn't say thanks? Or what if someone steps on your foot and just walks away? Don't you like it better when people say please, thank you, and excuse me? The Bible tells us to treat others the way we want to be treated. When we're kind and thoughtful to others, we show them respect. Showing respect lets others know we care about them and we want to do the right thing. And it makes God happy too!

THOUGHT OF THE DAY

What are three ways you can show respect to someone this week?

PRAY TODAY

Dear God, thank You for always treating me with kindness. Help me show respect to others too. Amen.

BEING BRAVE

"The Lord saved me from a lion and a bear. He will also save me from this Philistine."

1 SAMUEL 17:37A ICB

A s a boy, David prayed to God and trusted Him for help to be brave when he had to protect his sheep against lions and bears. Because David practiced trusting in God, he knew God could help him when he faced even bigger dangers. One day, a giant threatened to hurt Israel's army. David said he wasn't afraid to face the giant because he knew God would help him once again.

If you practice trusting God in small things every day, you won't have trouble being brave when big things come along!

THOUGHT OF THE DAY

Where do you need to ask God to help you be brave today?

PRAY TODAY

Dear God, thank You for always being with me. Please help me trust You more every day. Amen.

NEVER ALONE

"Be sure of this—that I am with you always, even to the end of the world."

MATTHEW 28:20B TLB

Do you ever feel alone? Maybe your best friend can't come over to play and you feel lonely. You may have to stay with a babysitter when your parents go to work or away for a while. These are all great times to remember that God is always with you.

The Bible tells us that God never leaves us. He is with us every single day and night, no matter where we are. Isn't that wonderful to know? Next time you are feeling lonely, remember these words from God: "I am with you always!"

THOUGHT OF THE DAY

God promises He'll never leave you—and He always keeps His promises!

PRAY TODAY

Dear God, I am so glad that You never leave me. Help me remember to ask You for help when I feel alone or afraid. Amen.

HE IS EVERYWHERE

God did this so that [people] would seek him and perhaps reach out for him and find him, though he is not far from any one of us.

ACTS 17:27 NIV

You can talk to God anytime you want to. That's because He's everywhere!

God isn't like you and me. He doesn't need to take a bike or car or airplane to get places. God is always with you, wherever you are. And He loves to hear from you! So turn to God anytime you feel afraid or discouraged. He is there. Praise Him when you feel thankful. He is there. Your whole life, no matter where you go or what you do, God will be right beside you. All you have to do is talk to Him!

THOUGHT OF THE DAY

You are never far away from God.

PRAY TODAY

Dear God, I love knowing that You are everywhere I go. Thank You for listening to all my prayers! Amen.

SMILE POWER!

Smiling faces make you happy, and good news makes you feel better.

PROVERBS 15:30 GNT

Did you know that you have a special power that can help people feel better? The Bible says that smiling faces and good news make you feel better. When you share a smile, a joke, or a funny story, you show you have a cheerful heart. And that makes others feel better. Maybe you can even sing one of Larry's silly songs to make a friend laugh! Look around and see who might need cheering up. Then use your "smile power" to help them feel better.

THOUGHT OF THE DAY

How can you cheer up a friend or someone in your family today?

PRAY TODAY

Dear God, thanks for giving me a cheerful heart. Help me to share some smiles today so others will feel better. Amen.

THE LIGHT ALWAYS WINS

The light shines in the darkness, and the darkness has never put it out.

JOHN 1:5 GNT

What happens when you shine a flashlight in a dark place? The darkness goes away! The Bible says that Jesus is the light of the world, and when we bring Him into a dark place, the darkness goes away.

When friends don't get along, things can seem dark. When someone is sad, that can also feel like a dark place. Ask Jesus to help you say kind words and show His love, bringing light into the dark places around you. When you choose to share God's light and love, the darkness goes away! The light of Jesus always wins!

THOUGHT OF THE DAY

The love of Jesus shines a light to make the darkest places bright!

PRAY TODAY

Dear God, thank You for being the light of the world. Please help me share Your light with others every day. Amen.

RUN FROM TEMPTATION

Run from temptations that capture young people. Always do the right thing.

2 TIMOTHY 2:22 CEV

Have you ever seen a magnet? If you move a nail close to a magnet, the nail will be pulled toward the magnet until it is stuck. Temptation is a lot like a magnet, pulling on us to do something we shouldn't. And the closer we get to doing or saying something wrong, the harder it is to pull away. Before we know it, we are stuck and in trouble! The Bible says that the best thing to do is to "run from temptations." Sometimes getting away is the best way to stay out of trouble!

THOUGHT OF THE DAY

Remember to run toward God and away from temptations!

PRAY TODAY

Dear God, I want to please You and not give in to temptation. Help me know when it's best to run away! Amen.

LOVE FORGIVES

Love is kind and patient, never jealous, boastful, proud, or rude. Love isn't selfish or quick-tempered. It doesn't keep a record of wrongs that others do.

1 CORINTHIANS 13:4–5 CEV

Sometimes when others say mean things, we want to say mean things right back to them. If they push ahead of us in line, we might feel like pushing them too. We want our own way. These kinds of things might feel right to us, but the Bible says that if we want to show love, we should forgive.

Forgiving someone means that we don't say angry words back, we don't push back, and we don't always have to have our own way. We treat others with kindness, just like we want to be treated. It's not easy, but God can help you!

THOUGHT OF THE DAY

How can you show love when someone hasn't been loving to you?

PRAY TODAY

Dear God, I'm so glad You always love and forgive me. Please help me remember to love and forgive others. Amen.

WORDS THAT HELP

Say only what is good and helpful to those you are talking to, and what will give them a blessing.

EPHESIANS 4:29B TLB

Have you ever thought about how your words can help someone else? Maybe a friend is feeling sad. You might say, "I hope you feel better soon." If you see someone without a toy, you could say, "Let's play together!" If your mom is very busy, you could ask, "What can I do to help?" These are all helpful words. They will bless others because these words show you care about how others are feeling. Think of other helpful words. How many people can you bless today?

THOUGHT OF THE DAY

Be a blessing every day by thinking of kind words to say!

PRAY TODAY

Dear God, please help me to be a blessing to others by using kind and helpful words today. Amen.

USE YOUR GIFTS

This is why I remind you to keep using the gift God gave you . . .

2 TIMOTHY 1:6 NCV

What do you like to do? Do you play an instrument or take dance classes? Maybe you draw pictures or you like to learn how things work. The special things you do are gifts from God. And He wants you to use your gifts well!

How can you use your gifts well? You can try to get better each day by practicing. If you like to sing, work hard to learn new songs. If you like to make up stories, try to learn new words to use each day. No one else has your special gifts. Be sure to use them!

THOUGHT OF THE DAY

How can you practice your gifts today?

PRAY TODAY

Dear God, thank You for the special gifts You've given me. Help me practice hard and use my gifts well. Amen.

DO IT NOW!

"All of us must quickly carry out the tasks assigned us by the one who sent me, for there is little time left before the night falls and all work comes to an end."

JOHN 9:4 TLB

What do you do when your mom asks you to pick up your toys? When you are playing outside and your dad calls you to come inside, do you come right away? When it's time for school, do you get your things together quickly so you're ready to go? When we each do our jobs quickly, then the whole family is happier. Waiting or whining just makes things take longer. Next time someone asks you to help out, see how fast you can get it done. If you do it now, you won't have to worry about doing it later!

THOUGHT OF THE DAY
It's much more fun to get things done!

PRAY TODAY
Dear God, I want to be a good worker. Please help me to do things right away instead of waiting. Amen.

CHOOSE YOUR WORDS

Be gracious in your speech. The goal is to bring out the best in others in a conversation, not put them down, not cut them out.

COLOSSIANS 4:6 MSG

Have you ever heard someone say, "Think before you speak"? That's because when you speak, you can really affect someone—you can choose to help, hurt, encourage, or ignore.

Use your words for good. When you speak, think about how you'd like people to talk to you. Offer praise for a job well done and encouragement in tough times. And when you talk about someone who is not there, be sure to follow the same rules. Speaking kindly is always the best choice. Don't be surprised if other people follow your example!

THOUGHT OF THE DAY

Once you speak, your words are out there and cannot be taken back. So choose words that make things better!

PRAY TODAY

Dear God, help me think before I speak. I want to choose words that make You and others happy! Amen.

IT'S WISE TO BE KIND

A kind person is doing himself a favor. But a cruel person brings trouble on himself.

PROVERBS 11:17 ICB

King Solomon was blessed with great wisdom. So when he talks about the benefits of kindness, like in the proverb above, you can be sure it's the wise choice!

Why do you think kindness is wise? Think about how you feel when you are kind to someone. How do you feel when you do something unkind? When you do something unkind, feelings get hurt, and you have to apologize. It's no fun. But when you show kindness to someone else, you both feel good! So follow King Solomon's advice and choose kindness every time.

THOUGHT OF THE DAY

Choose kindness in your actions and your words.

PRAY TODAY

Dear God, please help me to be wise like King Solomon, showing kindness to everyone, all the time! Amen.

GOD HAS A PLAN

"I know what I am planning for you," says the LORD. "I have good plans for you, not plans to hurt you. I will give you hope and a good future."

JEREMIAH 29:11 NCV

God is so excited about you! He made you to be very special, and He has big plans for you.

If God's making the plans, you can be sure they'll be great! He says that His plans will give you hope and a good future. God wants the very best for you. His plans might not look like your plans, but don't worry. Just keep talking to God and following His ways. And don't forget to practice all the wonderful gifts He's given you! That way, you'll be ready for everything God has in mind for you.

THOUGHT OF THE DAY

What do you want to be when you grow up?

PRAY TODAY

Dear God, please help me remember that Your plans are the best plans. Thank You for planning good things for me! Amen.

KNOW IT BY HEART

MOM OR DAD, HELP YOUR SON MEMORIZE THIS VERSE
AND TALK TO HIM ABOUT WHAT IT MEANS.

Rejoice in the Lord always.
Again I will say, rejoice!

—

PHILIPPIANS 4:4 NKJV

KNOW IT BY HEART

What then shall we say to these things?
If God is for us, who can be against us?

—

ROMANS 8:31 ESV

MOM OR DAD, HELP YOUR SON MEMORIZE THIS VERSE
AND TALK TO HIM ABOUT WHAT IT MEANS.

"God is the one who saves me.
I trust him. I am not afraid.
The Lord, the Lord, gives me strength
and makes me sing.
He has saved me."

—

ISAIAH 12:2 ICB

KNOW IT BY HEART

When Jesus spoke again to the people, he said, "I am the light of the world. Whoever follows me will never walk in darkness, but will have the light of life."

—

JOHN 8:12 NIV

KNOW IT BY HEART

*Be joyful in hope, patient in affliction,
faithful in prayer. Share with
the Lord's people who are in need.
Practice hospitality.*

—

ROMANS 12:12–13 NIV

KNOW IT BY HEART

He has shown you, O man, what is good;
*And what does the L*ORD *require of you*
But to do justly,
To love mercy,
And to walk humbly with your God?

—

MICAH 6:8 NKJV

KNOW IT BY HEART

MOM OR DAD, HELP YOUR SON MEMORIZE THIS VERSE
AND TALK TO HIM ABOUT WHAT IT MEANS.

*God so loved the world
that he gave his only Son,
so that everyone who believes in him
won't perish but will have eternal life.*

—

JOHN 3:16 CEB

KNOW IT BY HEART

MOM OR DAD, HELP YOUR SON MEMORIZE THIS VERSE
AND TALK TO HIM ABOUT WHAT IT MEANS.

The LORD is my strength and shield.
I trust him with all my heart.
He helps me, and my heart is filled with joy.
I burst out in songs of thanksgiving.

—

PSALM 28:7 NLT

KNOW IT BY HEART

MOM OR DAD, HELP YOUR SON MEMORIZE THIS VERSE
AND TALK TO HIM ABOUT WHAT IT MEANS.

Love each other like brothers and sisters.
Give your brothers and sisters more honor
than you want for yourselves.

—

ROMANS 12:10 ICB

KNOW IT BY HEART

*"Have I not commanded you?
Be strong and courageous.
Do not be afraid; do not be discouraged,
for the LORD your God will be
with you wherever you go."*

—

JOSHUA 1:9 NIV

KNOW IT BY HEART

MOM OR DAD, HELP YOUR SON MEMORIZE THIS VERSE
AND TALK TO HIM ABOUT WHAT IT MEANS.

*Love the LORD your God
with all your heart and with all your soul
and with all your strength.*

—

DEUTERONOMY 6:5 NIV